CATALOGING

**Recent Titles in
New Directions in Information Management**

CATALOGING

The Professional Development Cycle

Edited by
Sheila S. Intner
and
Janet Swan Hill

New Directions in Information Management, Number 26

Greenwood Press
New York • Westport, Connecticut • London

Library of Congress Cataloging-in-Publication Data

Cataloging : the professional development cycle / edited by Sheila S.
  Intner and Janet Swan Hill.
      p. cm.—(New directions in information management, ISSN
  0887-3844 ; no. 26)
    Includes bibliographical references and index.
    ISBN 0-313-27254-9 (alk. paper)
    1. Catalogers—Recruiting. 2. Catalogers—Training of.
  3. Catalogers—Education. 4. Library education. 5. Cataloging.
  6. Librarians. I. Intner, Sheila S. II. Hill, Janet Swan.
  III. Series.
  Z682.4.C38C38 1991
  331.12′4102—dc20   90-19797

British Library Cataloguing in Publication Data is available.

Library of Congress Catalog Card Number: 90-19797
ISBN: 0-313-27254-9
ISSN: 0887-3844

First published in 1991

Greenwood Press, 88 Post Road West, Westport, CT 06881
An imprint of Greenwood Publishing Group, Inc.

Printed in the United States of America

The paper used in this book complies with the
Permanent Paper Standard issued by the National
Information Standards Organization (Z39.48-1984).

10 9 8 7 6 5 4 3 2 1

CONTENTS

PART III: TRAINING CATALOGING LIBRARIANS

FIGURES

ACKNOWLEDGEMENTS

The editors wish to thank the Council on Library Resources for their generous support for the preparation of this book as well as for their funding of the Simmons College Symposium on Recruiting, Educating, and Training Cataloging Librarians: Solving the Problems, held in March of 1989, at which the discussions and new ideas contained in this book were first delivered as oral presentations. The symposium gave educators and practitioners an unusual opportunity to come together and consider issues fundamental to the profession.

The effectiveness of the discussions at the symposium that appear in this book were due in large measure to the excellent job of moderating them performed by Karen Muller and Janet Swan Hill, both of whom also helped to coordinate the symposium project with principal coordinator Sheila S. Intner. The editors appreciate their efforts.

Many others contributed to the success of the symposium, including William J. Holmes, president of Simmons College, and Robert D. Stueart, dean of the Graduate School of Library and Information Science of Simmons College. The symposium's smooth functioning and the comfort of the speakers and audience members were due to the combined efforts of many Simmons College administrators and staff members, especially those responsible for building services, media services, food services, and security.

Finally, this book would not have been possible without the assistance of Linda Willey, faculty secretary to the Graduate School of Library and Information Science, Simmons College, who faithfully transcribed the entire proceedings from ten hours of tape recordings supplied by the Simmons College Media Center.

EDITORS' INTRODUCTION

Cataloging: The Professional Development Cycle is intended for library educators, library managers, and other decision makers for libraries and their parent institutions, all of whom have a vital stake in the continued health of our libraries and the library profession. Although the focus here is mainly on cataloging librarians, the issues discussed in these pages are fundamental to the entire profession of librarianship. Will there be enough catalogers in the twenty-first century? Will new catalogers be sufficiently well-prepared? Are graduate catalogers preparing to fulfill the ongoing educational obligations undertaken by all professionals? Are libraries assisting these catalogers appropriately and accepting the staff development requirements that devolve upon all educational institutions? In each of these questions, one might substitute the word librarians for catalogers and the questions would be equally valid. There is no single answer to any of these questions, but, in the pages of this book, many answers are proposed as are expositions of the problems that the answers, themselves, raise.

Cataloging: The Professional Development Cycle contains edited versions of three free-for-all discussions during the Simmons College Symposium on Recruiting, Educating, and Training Cataloging Librarians held in Boston, Massachusetts in March of 1989. During these wide-ranging discussions, each following a series of formal presentations, the ideas presented for developing a new cadre of professional catalogers were explored, challenged, and evaluated by symposium participants and attendees, approximately 125 of them. In addition to the discussions, this book also contains those presentations or segments of presentations that were not included in the participants' formal papers and, therefore, did not appear in the symposium's original publication, *Recruiting, Educating, and Training Cataloging Librarians: Solving the Problems* (Greenwood Press, 1989), since that work contained papers prepared in advance of the event itself.

Symposium keynote speaker Robert M. Hayes set the pattern for the presentations by announcing that, since everyone could read his paper in *Recruiting, Educating, and Training Cataloging Librarians* distributed at the registration desk, he did not intend to talk about it at all. Instead, he chose to speak about other relevant topics he believed the assemblage should consider. Dr. Hayes' oral presentation is included here in its entirety.

Subsequently, several more speakers chose to do the same thing, abandoning their prepared texts in favor of expressing additional important ideas and viewpoints. Other speakers, taking advantage of the early deadline for their written papers, were able to move beyond their previously prepared texts to offer fresh data and/or new interpretations, made in a more considered fashion. Yale University's Maureen Sullivan, substituting for that institution's Karin Trainer who was unable to travel to Boston, gave an entirely different presentation of her own. All of their new material appears in this book.

A few speakers presented summaries of their prepared papers without adding new data. Their interesting and useful solutions may be found in *Recruiting, Educating, and Training Cataloging Librarians,* but they are not included here.

Cataloging: The Professional Development Cycle's three main sections correspond to the symposium's three sessions: Recruiting for Cataloging, Educating Catalogers, and On-the-job Training for

Catalogers. In each section, the discussions are preceded by edited versions of the oral presentations, which vary in length according to the amount of previously unrecorded data they contained. If the editors have concluded that the speaker's remarks might not be fully understood without reference to their prepared papers, an abstract of their chapter in *Recruiting, Educating, and Training Cataloging Librarians* has been provided.

The editors apologize in advance to all participants, both presenters and attendees, if, inadvertently, they have missed something important in editing their words or unknowingly mistaken a speaker's meaning. Working from spoken recordings puts the editors of the written words at somewhat of a disadvantage, but the editors have made every effort to be precise and accurate.

CATALOGING

Symposium keynote speaker Robert M. Hayes, whose distinguished career includes service for many years as dean and professor of the Graduate School of Library and Information Science at the University of California, Los Angeles, and two terms as chair of the American Library Association's Committee on Accreditation, holds global views of library and information science and the academic environment in which its graduate professional programs exist.

In his keynote address, Dr. Hayes asks a series of thought provoking questions and puts forward a number of challenging proposals for graduate library education that require the closest cooperation and integration of effort between educators and practitioners. The position of graduate library schools within academe is explored, as are methods for advancing that position to meet the needs of the modern information society. The role of the practitioner in the process is essential, creating a synergistic whole greater than the sum of its parts.

THE CHALLENGE OF EXCELLENCE IN LIBRARIANSHIP

ROBERT M. HAYES

There are some issues of importance in the development of excellence in library education that we ought to be considering. I shall identify a number of such issues in the hope that they will then be related to cataloging. The general context is: How can the library schools of the country with an objective of excellence combine their efforts and identify the needs and means for accomplishing excellence in library education? What are the issues with which they should be concerned? I would like to use this forum as a context in which to highlight some potential issues and hope that they may be considered in the symposium's subsequent deliberations.

A PRE-PROFESSIONAL CURRICULUM

The first issue I bring to your attention is especially appropriate because the symposium's first session is concerned with the problem of recruitment. The problem that I think we face in recruitment to our field, whether to cataloging or to any other aspect of it, is that librarianship is chosen as an alternative career. Too many students arrive at the doorsteps of library schools after completing undergraduate programs in which they had other objectives in mind. When they find, having gotten a bachelor's degree in, let us say, history, that they are not quite sure what they are going to do with it, they turn to librarianship as an alternative. I would like to have our field chosen by students when they start their undergraduate programs. The question is, how can we encourage them to do so?

I use as an analogy recommended curricula for pre-law, pre-medicine, and pre-other professional fields. And I ask, can we establish such a recommended undergraduate preparation for our field? I am not speaking of undergraduate courses in librarianship. Not at all. I am asking what undergraduate curriculum would best prepare students for entry to our field? Taking cataloging as a specific example, what undergraduate preparation would you want your students to have? Obviously, one type of desirable knowledge is language preparation. That implies to me that a recommendation for foreign language competence might be a component of a pre-library and information science curriculum.

What about linguistics? Logic? Or, mathematics, for example, as it relates to numerical taxonomy? Are these subjects that we should recommend students take if they wish to become catalogers? I have no direct answers. I present it to you as a question. I present it as a proposal.

What I visualize is that the catalog of Simmons College, of UCLA, of the University of Illinois, or of Louisiana State, or any college or university whether it is home to a graduate library program or not, will include in its undergraduate section a description for a pre-library/information science curriculum. It would indicate the courses we would urge students to take for entry to our field. My hope is that students beginning their undergraduate programs would see this description of undergraduate preparation for our field and say, "That is a field of interest to me." This interested student would design and follow a curriculum not only for getting a degree in history, but for developing the competencies in the undergraduate program that we have identified as desirable preparation for graduate professional study.

I present that as the first issue. As I have indicated, we have pre-law and pre-medicine as a means by which the student can prepare for entry into the professional programs in those fields. The question for cataloging is what would we like our students to come with by way of preparation so that they can take the greatest advantage of the library school curriculum?

A LIBRARY SCHOOL-TEACHING LIBRARY PARTNERSHIP

The second issue that I would like to raise reflects a wish on my part to develop a mechanism of cooperation between library schools and libraries. This mechanism of cooperation should be much closer and much more strongly developed than now exists, not only with academic libraries in particular, but more generally, with libraries of all kinds.

Most library schools have programs of internships in which students can gain some practical experience by working in a library. I am not referring to that. I am referring to a much stronger kind of partnership between library schools and libraries. The analogy I have in mind is that of the field of medicine, in which medical schools have teaching hospitals affiliated with them. The analogy, then, is of library schools with teaching libraries in partnership with them, in which major components of instruction are handled not by the library school, but in the library itself and by the professional staff of the library.

In my own experience in California, we have the advantage of a very, very strong University of California system with nine campuses, five of them within reach of UCLA in Southern California. Each of those campuses has staff with eminent qualifications for guiding students in many areas of professional practice. What I visualize is the possibility of partnerships between my own school and those campuses. Analogies could be found for Simmons College in the Boston area and, I suspect, in other communities, too.

There are immense challenges (I will not use the word "problems") in accomplishing such an objective, but I think that the benefits to be derived far outweigh the difficulties in meeting those challenges.

That is the second issue I would like to present to you, and I think it has immediate relevance for cataloging, because of the degree to which experience in professional practice may be significant in cataloging.

THE SCIENTIFIC FOUNDATION

That brings me to a third issue, a much more difficult and complicated one. If a partnership between library schools and libraries poses challenges, the next issue poses even deeper ones.

If I pursue the analogy of the medical school with the teaching hospital, I am faced with a very significant fact about education in the field of medicine: It is built upon a very strong basis in science. I am not using the word "science" with glowing lights. I am defining it as the discipline of organized knowledge. We have, in the medical education area, strong scientific bases, broadly applicable principles, whether these are in biology, chemistry, or in anatomy and physiology. Both professional practice of medicine and instruction in professional practice are built upon a very strong solid scientific basis. I present to you, therefore, the question: Can we create a comparable strong scientific or theoretical foundation for our field? (Perhaps we already have one, but believe me, it is not evident to me that we do.)

In no sense am I denigrating or denying the importance of professional practice; in fact, I regard it as absolutely critical. But I am asking whether there is a means to develop the science on which the professional practice instruction can be based. I am carefully avoiding, for very clear reasons, calling it "information science," because I am not identifying it with that in any sense. But, for example, could the area of numerican taxonomy and its application serve as a basis--a "science," if you will--for cataloging instruction? Are there other comparable scientific bases on which to build our education programs? The reason I wish to make this distinction is that I see the library school, in parallel to the school of medicine, being principally responsible for the instruction in that basic science component. Not totally, but principally.

And, in that school-library partnership, I see the teaching library as taking a strong responsibility in the area of professional practice instruction. So, I have in mind a vision and I present to you the question: Firstly, is this an appropriate vision; and secondly, in the area of cataloging in particular, can we identify basic science components that can be taught independently of professional practice, but on which professional practice instruction can then be built?

THE RESEARCH BASE

And so we come to another critical issue: How do we end our isolation from the rest of the campus community? It is a distinct drawback that faculty in library and information science find themselves in relative isolation from the remainder of the academic enterprise. This is disadvantageous in several respects. Perhaps most directly, it has a negative impact on their political power within the campus. But, secondly, it may dimish the quality and character of the instructional program itself. As long as the library school is isolated, and out of the mainstream of academic departments, it has little impact upon them, and the programs of other departments or of the parent institution have little impact upon the library school.

I raise the question, what can we do to strengthen those ties, and, in particular, are there aspects of cataloging which would especially strengthen them? Are there tools we have and use that would have value in archeology or in the fine arts, in music or in the sciences? Clearly there are, and I am not just speaking of the practice of librarianship in those fields. I am speaking of the potential significance that the science of librarianship and the practice of cataloging may have to those fields as well.

One example that illustrates the value and the challenges of applying the science of cataloging to other fields is the management of digitized image files, an issue that is a particular immediate concern of mine. Today digitized image files are becoming important throughout the university, in every area of teaching and research, from medicine to the fine arts, from archeology and engineering to architecture and urban planning, from physics and chemistry to biology. The use of the process of digital visualization, the acquisition of data about the human body and about the world through the observation of natural phenomena, these are generating files of truly immense size. Researchers throughout the university face the very serious problem of how to manage those files. How should they be cataloged? How should their content be indexed? How should access to them be provided? I raise the question, which I hope is worthy of consideration, "What can cataloging contribute to answering those needs in each of the several areas in which digitized images are becoming important?"

THE IMPACT OF INFORMATION POLICY

Another issue of importance, which perhaps is not as intimately related to cataloging as some of the others I have mentioned, although I would be interested in your reaction to it, is the area of information policy. I raise this issue, therefore, not because it is related specifically to the issues of this symposium, but because it certainly is related to the context of library education in general. How do we integrate into library education issues related to information policies, telecommunications policies, and the whole range of political decisions with respect to the allocation of resources to our field? It is by no means easy to do so.

At UCLA, we have been making a conscious effort to integrate attention to information policy into our curriculum with, I hope, some success, but not without problems. It reminds me, for very obvious reasons, of my own situation some twenty-five or thirty years ago, when I had the task of bringing a concern with the application of computers to my colleagues in library education. I can assure you that, at that time, it was by no means evident that computers had applications in libraries. Some of you may recall a series of exchanges, one of them an article by Ellsworth Mason, in which he used the phrase, "The great gas bubble prik't" in referring to library automation.[1] My name was the only individual's name mentioned in that article. You might be interested in the response of some of my faculty: They went around after that article was published mumbling "the Emperor's clothes."

It was not easy to bring automation into library education, even in schools where there was some degree of receptivity to it, but developments in the quarter century since then have demonstrated clearly that it is meaningful to library education. In the same vein, we face comparable barriers in trying to incorporate concerns with the political and technical aspects of information and telecommunications policies into our curriculum. How can they be overcome? I think it is important that we do so, for I believe that, in future decades, this area will be as important to our field as automation has been over the past two or three decades.

---

[1] Ellsworth Mason, "The Great Gas Bubble Prik't," *College & Research Libraries* 32:183-96 (May 1971)

FACULTY RECRUITMENT

A final issue I wish to raise is: How do we recruit faculty from a diversity of disciplines and integrate those faculty into our schools? Many of the objectives I have identified should draw on faculty from a wide range of academic departments-- mathematicians, psychologists, economists, engineers, as well as historians and people from literature and from library science. Nor, in raising this as a question, am I in any way trying to diminish the importance of library schools in preparing faculty; I think we have excellent faculty coming from library schools. But, I want to know how we can bring greater diversity of faculty to our schools. I raise this question with specific reference to the area of cataloging. Are there disciplines on which we should draw in educating cataloging students, or, of necessity, must catalogers come solely from the discipline of library and information science?

SEEKING ANSWERS

These then are the issues I wish to raise with you:
(1) Design of an undergraduate preparation, a pre-library and information science curriculum akin to existing pre-medicine and pre-law curricula;
(2) Development of a library school-teaching library partnership similar to the medical school-teaching hospital partnership;
(3) Identification of the scientific foundations for our field;
(4) Expansion of our research base;
(5) Integration of library school faculty and research with other disciplines and assumption of a position in the mainstream of the university;
(6) Incorporation of information policy concerns into the library and information science curriculum; and, finally,
(7) Increase in the diversity of library school faculty by recruiting faculty members from relevant disciplines other than librarianship.

These are the issues I hope will spark discussion and debate. I have raised them not because I have answers to them or, even, because I hold firm positions on them. I have, in some instances, dreams, wishes, and hopes for certain outcomes, but they are not necessarily outcomes to which I am irrevocably committed. Rather, these are questions and issues that I believe should be explored and that I myself will be exploring for as many years as I can. I raise them with you at this symposium, because I think they may stimulate lines of thought with specific relation to cataloging and because of the significance these issues may have to your special field of interest.

PART I

RECRUITING CATALOGING LIBRARIANS

James M. Matarazzo, Professor and former Associate Dean of the Graduate School of Library and Information Science at Simmons College, led off the symposium's first session, Recruiting Cataloging Librarians, with a session keynote address. During his fourteen year deanship, Dr. Matarazzo was responsible for recruitment, admissions, student affairs, and placement. Among his innovations was a job hotline, a network operating throughout New England, twenty-four hours a day, seven days a week, to match librarians seeking positions with librarians seeking to employ them. The hotline alerted Dr. Matarazzo to increasingly intense efforts to hire catalogers and he sought explanations for the combination of factors that led to the shortage.

Dr. Matarazzo examined studies conducted by the U.S. Bureau of Labor Statistics and King Research in 1970 and 1980, respectively, that projected a declining need for librarians in future years.[1] He claimed that, perhaps in response to the projections (although figures used by both research teams actually were in error), the number of library school graduates began to decline in 1978 and were continuing to decline in 1989. Dr. Matarazzo showed that, based on new census data not available to the Bureau or to the King researchers, it was fair to anticipate a need for 70,000 new librarians in the next decade, a figure that cannot even begin to be matched by graduates from library schools. Dr. Matarazzo offered two explanations for the current shortage and two solutions to the problem.

THE RECRUITMENT MUDDLE: ENTRANCES AND EXITS

JAMES M. MATARAZZO

---

[1] U.S. Bureau of Labor Statistics, *Library Manpower: A Study of Demand and Supply* (Washington, D.C.: U.S. Government Printing Office, 1975); and King Research, *Library Human Resources: A Study of Supply and Demand* (Chicago: American Library Association, 1983).

In most instances we use research to help us solve problems, putting our faith in statistics that appear to reflect systematic data gathering and careful analysis. The 1970 Bureau of Labor Statistics study and the 1980 King Research study both suggested a decline in the need for librarians. Nevertheless, there has been an increase in recruiting intensity for many specialties, while there was simultaneously a decline in the number of entering professionals.

THE ENTRANCES

What happened, I believe, is that practitioners, while they probably did not wade through each of these two influential reports, captured their generalizations in little snippets from summaries and commentaries appearing in *American Libraries* and *Library Journal*. Saying to themselves, "It doesn't look like there is going to be much need for people to work in libraries," those practitioners began, in my judgment, referring fewer and fewer students to library schools. And, even though the number of vacancies being posted between 1980 and 1987 doubled, at least as seen from the Simmons College-based New England job hotline, interest was not sparked in what I think is probably the most effective means for recruitment: Individual librarian referral. Librarians generally spot the bright young people who come to work in libraries and encourage them to pursue their interest by going to library school.

Nancy Van House, who wrote the first part of the King Report that dealt with salaries as well as doing subsequent studies of librarians' earning power,[2] pointed out a correlation between starting salaries and the number of MLS degrees. Not surprisingly, Van House showed there were more librarians when librarians were paid better. As librarians' salaries in real dollars declined, so did their numbers. Those who came into the profession in the 1960s

---

[2] Nancy A. Van House, "MLS Delivers a Poor Payoff on Investment,"*American Libraries* 16 (Sept. 1985);548-51.

and 1970s, came in during the best salary times. While librarians might earn more dollars per year now, there is not much they can do with the additional money because the dollars cannot buy as much any more. (This is similar to what has happened to Snickers bars. They are the same size they've always been, but they used to cost a nickel and now they are forty-five cents. The price of the Snickers bar has gone up nine times, but our salaries have not.)

Thus, two factors contributed heavily to the current shortage of librarians: First, fewer candidates were being recruited into librarianship in response to recommendations of both the Bureau of Labor Statistics and the King studies--representing the authoritative knowledge of a federal government agency and a well-respected information research firm--i.e., to shrink or redirect the library labor force in the future; and, second, the dollars-and-cents value of library work was declining.

THE EXITS

Van House does not feel that salary is the only reason that people become librarians, nor do I. However, I agree with her that it is a variable that ought to be considered. Clearly, if Van House's research is accurate and there is a correlation between real income levels and the number of librarians that we appear to be graduating from library schools, one simple answer to the recruitment problem for new catalogers is to raise the salaries of catalogers.

There also is, in my judgment, a correlation between how encouraged we are about the profession in relation to our own salaries that affects how we reach out to those student assistants or college graduates who work for us so willingly and so well, to say "You ought to become a librarian."

That is exactly what happened to me. My boss was a keen recruiter, not only with me, but with every student who worked in his very small library. The library held just 36,000 volumes and he was the only professional staff member. There were two other full time people and the rest were students who worked part time. Every single student was poked and prodded to think about librarianship as a career. And I think I now know why my boss was happy about his position at the time. In 1965, my boss was making the equivalent of $50,000. in today's dollars.

What is the relationship between what one is paid and how one feels about the profession? Might this relationship parallel that between what librarians are paid and how many people wish to enter the field? If one accepts that these factors might be linked, then practitioner referrals are one of the essential processes through which the linkage functions.

As things currently stand, all of the library schools in the United States graduating all of the students they currently graduate cannot replace the librarians who will retire by the year 2000. There is no way to come up with the requisite number of new workers with the programs now in place. In addition, we must remember that eleven or twelve library schools have closed since the Bureau of Labor Statistics did its first study. Furthermore, from the ages of librarians in 1980, we can predict that 30,000 more will retire by the year 2010 and that 34,000 more will retire by the year 2020. Thus, in the next thirty-one years, three-quarters of the labor force that was working in 1980 will retire. In 1970, the Bureau of Labor Statistics said 47,000 would retire by 1985. In my paper, "Recruitment: The Way Ahead,"[3] I demonstrated that at least 70,000 would retire by 2000 and 64,000 more by 2020. The Bureau of Labor Statistics also claimed that and additional 121,000 people, who did not retire, would leave the field by 1985 due to death, change of occupation, leave of absence from active status, etc. My statistics do not include any allowance for people who will leave the field other than for retirement. The figure for persons leaving the field is one that

---

[3] James M. Matarazzo, "Recruitment: The Way Ahead," in *Recruiting, Educating, and Training Cataloging Librarians: Solving the Problems,* edited by Sheila S. Intner and Janet Swan Hill (Westport, Conn.: Greenwood Press, 1989), 19-38

could be on the rise, especially if salaries for people in practice do not increase.

SALARY ISSUES

While it is important to consider more than starting salaries, starting salaries for new professionals are the primary issue here, because they are the focus of recruitment to the field.

Most librarians in the United States have earned master's degrees. We must assume that students who elect to take master's degree programs think carefully about their choices, just as you and I think carefully when we refer people to library schools in the United States or in Canada. It is reasonable then, to ask how their starting salaries would compare with a number of other fields for which a master's degree might or might not be required. Figure 1 shows starting salaries for a variety of positions offered to master's degree candidates as of July 1988.[4] The salary level for social scientists (an umbrella term which can be interpreted to include librarians) is several thousand dollars below their nearest rivals.

What about the longer view? The people who contemplate earning library degrees can see the same salaries that I saw in the November 1988 issue of *American Libraries* which, for example, listed $29,392. as the annual salary for an experienced librarian working as head of a branch or a department.[5] This is what recent master's degree recipients are earning several years after earning their degrees. I think it has affected the number of people who elect to come into this profession's master's degree programs. Not only is there a discrepancy among starting salaries, but also among potential

---

[4] Statistics of the type represented in figure 1 are collected quarterly by the College Placement Council and reported to their placement offices. Figure 1 contains the July 1988 report from 187 placement offices at 154 U.S. colleges. I do not know whether they are scientifically drawn, but they do represent a geographic distribution.

[5] Mary Jo Lynch, "ALA Publishes 1988 Salary Data," *American Libraries 19* (Nov. 1988):887-88.

incomes after professionals have worked ten or fifteen years in the field.   Moen's study of library school students showed the average student profile to be thirty-six years old, and married, with two children.[6]   What might prospective candidates think who wish to own their own homes, who wish to own their own automobile, who wish to send their children to college--public or private?   They are looking at these figures, too.

The same sort of comparison can be made by measuring salaries against the consumer price index, this time taking the highest salaries. The highest starting salaries for librarians often are paid in the corporate library sector; yet, comparing the highest salaries paid beginning librarians in special libraries with the national consumer price index shows a negative gap that has been widening since the early 1970s.

Even the highest starting salaries in the library field have not kept up with the consumer price index, although this may be true for other professions, too. Many people are having difficulty keeping up with the actual worth of the dollar, i.e., the dollar in relation to the things we would like to buy.

We are in competition with other fields in attracting new members, so those who run libraries, those who influence the people who run libraries, might start (in my judgment) at the most basic level: getting salaries up. They must work not just to get starting salaries up, but also the salaries being earned by department heads and associate department heads. Perhaps the department heads will begin to feel better about what they do, the way my boss felt better about what he did. Seventy percent of the students in library school today claimed to have been influenced by librarians in deciding to come to library school. At least thirty percent of the students I have interviewed recently have been told not to go to library school by librarians.

---

6 William E. Moen, "Library and Information Science Student Attitudes, Demographics and Aspirations Survey: Who We Are and Why We Are Here," in *Librarians for The New Millenium* (Chicago: American Library Association, 1988), p. 91-109

A related problem I have encountered personally is a secret glee over the shortage of librarians on the part of working professionals. At a 1988 recruitment program sponsored by the American Library Association's Office of Library Personnel Resources in New Orleans, the speakers may have been whipped up into a frenzy to influence those who attended to recruit for the profession, but what I heard whispered all around the tables was, "Good, I'm glad there is a shortage. Salaries will rise."

Unfortunately, the fact that there is a shortage of librarians does not mean salary increases will follow immediately. It took salaries sixteen years to increase from the 1950s to the 1960s before there was a measurable impact on enrollment. Another thirty percent of today's librarians will retire sixteen years hence. We cannot wait for the salaries to catch up; the salary issue must be forced now.

From an economic standpoint, Van House might conclude in her next study that, with present salary conditions, even if one is offered a free library degree, it is not worth accepting.

SOLUTIONS

The two solutions I suggest are closely related: First and most important, all salaries must go up, and quickly; and second, librarians must begin to express the enthusiasm they feel for their jobs, and seek actively to extend their interest and excitement to the young people around them.

CONCLUSIONS

Library and information science is a very interesting field, and the people who practice it are equally interesting. At cocktail parties, however, I have seen librarians give all sorts of convoluted excuses rather than admit their chosen profession. It would be simpler to say, "I am a librarian and I like it. Perhaps you have never really talked to a librarian before in a serious one-to-one conversation where you don't want a fine waived, but here is your chance. What do you want to ask me? What do you want to know?"

Still more important, the next time the supply of new librarians just about matches the demand for them, do not tell the Bureau of Labor Statistics that a study must be conducted, because every single graduate of every library school in the country does not receive an ideal job offer thirty seconds after receiving his or her diploma. Even in a surplus state, or in a so-called surplus state (since 1970 there have never been real surpluses), jobs have been available in some areas of the country, but students have been unwilling to go to those areas and take those jobs. Thus, even when we solve the overall balance of supply and demand, localized supply problems will remain. Most of the students who go to library school do not exhibit much mobility. After all, only about three percent leave their state to go to library school. How mobile they might be after receiving their diplomas is another question, but it is something worth pondering.

Twenty-three years ago, I earned the national average starting salary in my first professional library position. It was not a lot of money and I will not tell you how much it was. You would not believe it anyway, the world has changed so much in twenty-three years. My Snickers bar was still a nickel then. Today, that position should pay, to start, $33,635. So, we have to work on that. Next, all of your salaries must be doubled, so the same thing that happened to me will begin to happen to you. You will spot wonderful young people out there and, because you will be comfortable with your own salary, you will say to them, "You ought to go to library school."

The library schools will fill up again. But, this time be careful not to say, "Gee, I have two applicants for this position; I don't know which one to pick. Why do they graduate so many librarians?"

FIGURE 1

MASTER'S CANDIDATES, AVERAGE ANNUAL OFFERS

<u>Business</u>

Accounting	27,480
MBA - Non tech <1 year	33,492
MBA - Tech <1 year	38,304
MS - Business	31,296
Administration	26,172
Bank & Finance	37,596
Industrial Management	34,128
Lab/Ind. Relations	31,368
MIS	31,680

<u>Social Sciences</u>   23,040

<u>Engineering</u>

Aerospace & Aeronautical	34,116
Bioengineering & Biomedical	41,004
Chemical	34,452
Civil (incl. Construction, Sanitary, & Transportation Engineering)	29,604
Electrical	36,096
Geological	28,308
Industrial	33,300
Mechanical	34,080
Metallurgical	34,044
Nuclear	31,860
Chemistry	31,968
Computer Science	34,392
Geology & Related Geological Sciences	29,856
Mathematics	29,352
Physics	38,328

Source: *CPC Salary Survey, July 1988*

The College Placement Council surveys a consistent population of 187 placement officers at 154 colleges and universities throughout the United States.

FIGURE 2

CPI AND LIBRARIAN SALARIES

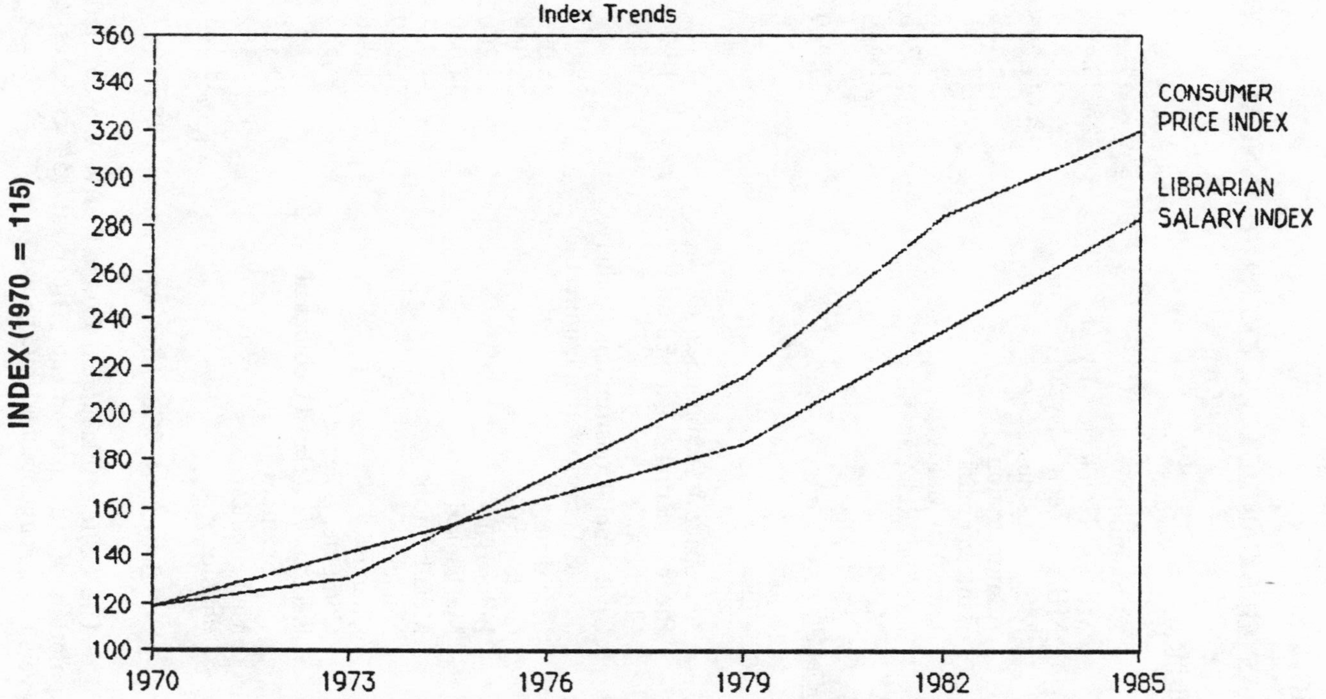

Index Trends

CONSUMER PRICE INDEX

LIBRARIAN SALARY INDEX

INDEX (1970 = 115)

360 340 320 300 280 260 240 220 200 180 160 140 120 100

1970 1973 1976 1979 1982 1985

Source: Special Libraries Association Annual and Triennial Salary Surveys

FIGURE 3

RELATIONSHIP BETWEEN DEFLATED STARTING SALARIES AND ACCREDITED MLS DEGREES, 1950-1980

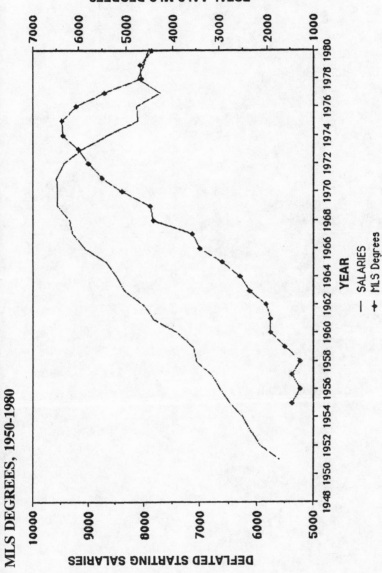

Source: Library Human Resources, 1983. A merger of data
         in two tables into one by James M. Matarazzo

Eight speakers followed session keynoter Matarazzo, addressing various problems of recruiting cataloging librarians. Among the themes that kept recurring were emphases on the changing skills needed by cataloging librarians, the ability of transporting traditional cataloging skills to non-traditional job descriptions, and the need to develop more effective recruiting strategies. Each of the speakers offered insights into these issues and gave suggestions for potential solutions to the shortage of catalogers. Their remarks are brought together here.

RECRUITING: ANALYSES AND STRATEGIES

LIZ BISHOFF, Manager, Cataloging and Database Services, OCLC, Inc.

Many of you know that I have a seventeen-year-old boy, and when he was about ten or eleven, we were having one of these "What do I want to be when I grow up?" conversations. We went through fireman, policeman, attorney, doctor--my mother wants him to be a doctor. When he was three he told her, "Grandma, first I'm going to be Superman, then I'm going to be a doctor." But, I finally got to, "Well, what about being a librarian?" and he replied, "They work too hard and they don't make enough money."

I hate to admit it, but I think that is true. I'm tired of doing two jobs because I have vacancies, and many of us could ask directors who want us to take on multiple jobs, "What duties do you want me to drop if I assume this new responsibility?"

Although everyone bemoans the shortage of catalogers, most particularly they express concern over the lack of well qualified catalogers. I think this is due in large part to changes in needed qualifications. We now need catalogers who have, in addition to the usual skills and knowledge, competencies in languages and nonbook media as well as technological know-how and strong management and leadership skills.

In part, this is due to the fact that the computerized cataloging networks, such as OCLC and RLIN, have increased the availability of cataloging copy so that paraprofessionals can handle routine editing of existing cataloging data. While this has reduced the amount of original cataloging that needs to be done, it has made the remaining original work far more specialized and difficult. In libraries that have not computerized beyond the stage of using a cataloging network for technical processing by staff members, catalogers continue to perform their traditional roles as original catalogers, department managers, and staff trainers, but they do so in a more sophisticated environment and with a different mix of professional and nonprofessional staff.

We also have seen an increased demand for catalogers' skills in other areas of librarianship. Skills in organizing information are the same as those required for information system design and analysis. Libraries initiating or implementing computer system projects are looking to attract the same group of people to conduct needs analyses, select local computer systems, and manage their operations as are libraries who need original catalogers. Non-library employers, such as computer system vendors, publishers, and bibliographic networks, also require the catalogers' expertise and knowledge. Catalogers now are filling positions in these non-library enterprises, doing system design, user support, product development, sales, and project management.

Today's requirements for catalogers have expanded dramatically since the 1960s, and position descriptions in the library press ask for knowledge of MARC formats, experience with bibliographic sources, local systems, systems analysis techniques, and technical service management in addition to AACR2R, LCRIs, LCSH, DDC, or LCC. It is a good thing that it is people in the profession who read these ads, because the acronyms for cataloging rules, etc. would befuddle anyone else.

Because our requirements are expanding and diversifying, so must our recruiting efforts. We can no longer expect to succeed by just posting positions at the American Library Association conferences, or advertising in professional journals. Recruiting techniques may involve campus visits, more and better job advertisements, posters in local libraries to attract people, brochures, open-houses, use of executive search firms for senior positions, and, of course, the ever-reliable word of mouth. Many outside forces, such as salaries and mobility, impact our recruiting abilities, so we also need to look at affirmative action and equal employment opportunity requirements, civil service programs, and the problems of relocation for members of a female dominated profession.

Campus recruiting to attract students to cataloging should begin well before students are nearing the completion of their professional education. We need to talk to them when they are working in our libraries, when they are undergraduate students, even when they are high school pages. We certainly need to talk to them in the summer or fall before they begin their program of study. We need to explain to students the kinds of opportunities that are available and what they need to do to prepare for them. Last April, for example, I visited the University of Kentucky. Professor Lois Mai Chan was very accommodating, and allowed me to talk to her Advanced Cataloging class about different opportunities in cataloging. I was absolutely astounded to discover that these students, who were getting ready to graduate in a month, believed cataloging job opportunities occurred only in academic libraries, and that, to be successful in obtaining them, they had to have a science background and a second language. As a former public library technical services administrator, I was aghast. No wonder public libraries can't find any catalogers. No wonder we can't find anybody to do system design at OCLC, because students' views of cataloging are so narrow.

Another example: While I was still working at a public library, I had a practicum student who asked me in some dismay (and I am not exaggerating), "Do you mean librarians have to talk to people?"

I said, "Well, where do you think librarians get the questions they answer?"

She didn't know. All she saw was that the librarian answered the question. She, too, was at the end of her academic career. When I contacted the library school, they told me that there was nothing they could do about her. This student had been accepted into the program and she would graduate. At that moment, I wished for an electronic bulletin board on which I could post a message, "Don't hire this person."

Employers cannot wait until students are about to graduate to begin informing them about the real world. We need to establish relationships with library schools that involve us both with students and educators. If Lois knows the kinds of vacancies I need to fill at OCLC, or at Columbus Public Library, or at Ohio State University, she can do a better job of guiding students to me. I want Lois's best students channelled directly to me, because I want to hire the best students.

And we cannot depend only on relationships with the library schools in our area. First, not all of us have a local library school. Second, one school cannot meet all our needs. I was very interested to see this spring, that staff from the Los Angeles County Public Library were being sent as far east as Indiana University to do on-campus recruiting.

We also need to look at new ways to recruit during conferences. During the recent LITA conference in Boston, a number of key institutions in the Boston area held open houses. They were advertised in the conference program just like new product demonstrations by Gaylord, Baker & Taylor, or one of the local computer systems vendors. "Come to an open house and find out what jobs we have."

To highlight our staff needs and the types of functions and tasks they involve, OCLC designed some brochures. At every meeting and discussion group I attend, I just hand them out or put them on the tables. Maybe somebody will pick them up and contact me. OCLC traditionally has recruited librarians with extensive cataloging and MARC format experience. Lately, we find we cannot fill our positions with this expertise, so we ask: Can we hire generalist catalogers? Can we hire recent graduates with extensive paraprofessional experience? Can we establish a "grow your own" environment similar to the on-the-job training environment used by many large banks and businesses? This would allow us to hire recent graduates and train them for our particular needs. Unfortunately, we have not been able to implement such a program yet, but I am still pursuing it.

These are some assertive recruiting ideas to solve the current shortage. More importantly, I think we need to develop recruiting programs to prevent the present situation from recurring. The supply of new catalogers is insufficient not only for today, but also for the future. Today's deficit will result in an insufficient pool of qualified managers, senior designers, and trainers in the next five to ten years. Today's solutions represent an investment that goes far beyond today's problems.

D. WHITNEY COE, Anglo-American Bibliographer, Princeton University.

Two ways in which the Princeton University Library has been able to recruit new catalogers successfully have been to develop them from the ranks of library support staff and to establish relationships with nearby library schools. Princeton is fortunate in having not just one, but several library schools within a reasonable geographic radius as well as a flexible benefits program that allows for generous tuition benefits. Thus, within the last few years, three cataloging positions were filled by encouraging non-degreed support staff to complete their master's degrees while working. In addition, two of three student-interns were hired upon completing their degrees.

The success of these programs at Princeton is attributable to a combination of administrative flexibility and attention to people as individuals. Our cataloging department, which is divided into teams, does not have to hold a vacancy open indefinitely. Depending on the nature of the librarians' special knowledge, staffing reassignments may open up different and more promising recruitment opportunities when a search for someone with particular skills fails. Personnel strategies are flexible, too, and job descriptions have been revised to make them more attractive.

A great deal of care and attention is paid to getting to know potential colleagues. Candidates for professional positions have day-long interviews that include meeting as many people as possible and seeing as much of library operations as time allows. Even student-interns are interviewed, to ensure that there is a good match between the opportunities being offered by the library and the person's goals and objectives.

The personal nature of recruitment is visible at Princeton in several ways. First, each of us brings his or her own personality and skills to the task. Many people are involved in a search for a new cataloger, including, always, the team leader for whom the prospective candidate will work. Second, each candidate is evaluated in terms of what he or she can bring to the positions and the division in general, and not necessarily to fit a preconceived pattern exactly. Third, our contacts with people are made in a variety of ways, including those already mentioned as well as bringing library school classes to visit the library, inviting students to participate in local professional association events, and, occasionally, acting as adjunct lecturers for a local library school. In each of these activities, our interest in new professionals is to assist them in their education and develop a positive process of entry to the profession, not just to fill positions. This can be turned into a positive situation for everyone involved.

ELIZABETH FUTAS, Director, Graduate School of Library and Information Studies, and Acting Dean, Graduate School of Arts and Sciences, University of Rhode Island.

Fay Zipkowitz and I are the only educators at this symposium who are making a presentation focused on recruiting. We want to reach further back in the professional development cycle than those who preceded us, to a point before the library professional looks at job, before library school students consider career choices, to discuss a program we at the University of Rhode Island promote. It is a program of outreach from the library school to the library community, and beyond the workplace to the world at large.

Three of us conduct the recruiting program, and all of us are practitioners who wound up in library education. We recruited people to the profession when we were in practice--two of my student aides ended up becoming librarians--so perhaps it is natural that we are the ones who do what we call our dog-and-pony show. Coincidentally, all of us are related to cataloging. I trained to be a cataloger in a special library, although my last job in practice was as a reference librarian in an academic library; Fay also is a former cataloger who teaches our beginning cataloging course; and our third colleague teaches nonprint cataloging. We are a perfect trio. Fay and I both decided to become librarians at the age of six and, subsequently, never changed our minds. We come from almost the same neighborhood in Brooklyn, although we did not know each other then. Perhaps there is something in the air. We still would rather be librarians than anything else.

I never worked in a library before I went to library school, but most people I know did. Also, most people I know who went to library school had a librarian that they knew well, a relative or a family friend. When I first started teaching at Rutgers and, later, at Emory, I would ask my required classes: "How many of you have librarians in your family or among close family friends?" The answer usually was around two-thirds of the class. It began to bother me that so many had known librarians before coming into the profession. So I stopped asking the question. But the better strategy, I now think, is to take advantage of this knowledge and furnish every potential candidate with an inviting role model.

We three University of Rhode Island faculty members get together for our recruiting forays on Saturdays, usually twice a term. We go out to libraries, pour coffee and serve cake, and talk to people, both on an individual and a group basis. Thus far, we have been to Portsmouth, Worcester, and Amherst, and we are arranging to do another appearance in Amherst and one in Boston. We recruit among the libraries' communities and support staff in accordance with the American Library Association slogan, "Each One Reach One". We always are very happily received and these coffees appear to interest people in becoming professionally-trained librarians or, if they are already there, in being more active within the profession.

A second place we recruit is in our university, and I must admit of all the recruiting we do, it is the least successful. Every spring, the University of Rhode Island holds a college fair for high school students, who come with their parents for a weekend of frolic. Like the other schools and departments, we set up a nice table with glossy brochures that the American Library Association kindly sends us, and buttons and various other information pieces. We set up this beautiful table and everybody runs around to the computer science table and the history table, while we sit alone. That's the bad news-- we wind up sitting alone a lot. The good news is that we have learned how to sit alone and not look lonely. We manage to look inviting. We do it by taking along a number of our students and having a number of faculty there, so we enjoy talking to one another. Then, we draw in the people who wander by looking for computer science.

At the college fairs, we seem to appeal mostly to the parents of seventeen-year-olds. Noticing this led me to conclude that one of librarianship's real problems is that it is a second career for a good many people. They enter our field when they reach their thirties and forties--not in their twenties; and, if they start out in their mid-to-late thirties or forties, they have fewer years to work. I hypothesize that librarians reach 65 sooner, on average, than people in other professions, because they start later in life. There is bound to be an important impact on the profession in having so many members with fewer productive years. If librarianship were the first career choice, we could expect thirty to forty years of active service; if it is the second, that estimate drops, often to as little as ten or fifteen years.

Recruiting high school students is not the primary reason we sit at college fairs, although we are happy to get them. We sit there so the rest of the university sees us, and so parents and other people see us, and we gain a visibility that we might not achieve any other way. That helps to ensure the survival of the library school and, who knows, it might even recruit a few seventeen-year-olds to the field.

FAY ZIPKOWITZ, Associate Professor, University of Rhode Island.

Based on comments already made and studies mentioned, many people choose our field based on their experiences working in libraries. Even though we do not know exactly what precipitates those decisions, we assume it is some kind of positive experience they have had. Perhaps some people can make an intellectual leap past a negative experience and maybe some will accept that a more challenging set of activities than they have found may be out there, but I think that is a very large leap to expect. I think it is fair to conclude that the settings in which people find themselves are going to affect their choices. In cataloging, we find a real contradiction between what we communicate in our recruiting and teaching and what students see in their present or previous positions. Catalogers' not-so-happy status in the workplace steers students away from making the choice to go into cataloging.[1]

---

[1] Evidence of catalogers' negative status is offered by Herbert S. White in one of his "White Papers," *Library Journal* 112 (April 1, 1987): 48-49 .

What we can do to address the problem is to concentrate on the value of catalogers' skills and expand their horizons beyond the tasks students may be performing in their paraprofessional positions. We can try to get them more involved in discussion of career possibilities in the organizational setting. Also we as catalogers have to look at the image we present to others, how we view our work, and the attitudes we broadcast about it. Students see catalogers the way they are, not the way they would like to be seen. We should view ourselves as professionals who know and remember who and what the library is for and strive to keep that mission in front of us. We should display our concern with issues and trends in all areas of the field and discuss these intelligently with our staffs. We should be involved with research and share our research with them. We can and we should demonstrate leadership, responsiveness to challenge, concern about developing and maintaining standards, and willingness to direct and accept change.

Libraries will have to improve the workplace to make the reality live up to the promises made to potential catalogers by educators and recruiters. Opportunities to get involved in policy formulation processes and other interdisciplinary activities need to be provided for technical services staff to demonstrate that catalogers do more than just sit around and catalog. If I stress standards, intellectual activity, goal orientation, growth, and service in my classroom, but students see drudgery, defensiveness, and territorial turf wars, or people who appear to have lost sight of their professional objectives in the library, they will shy away from finding themselves in what they perceive as dead-end, menial kinds of positions.

We catalogers need to feel better about ourselves and what we do. And, more importantly, we need to broadcast that message to potential catalogers.

HEIDI LEE HOERMAN, Doctoral student, School of Library and Information Science, Indiana University; formerly Assistant Dean for Technical Services, Montana State University.

In three successive issues of *Library Journal* last fall, there were advertisements for three different positions desiring horticultural backgrounds, and countless advertisements asking for biological and life sciences backgrounds. A National Agricultural Library (NAL) recruiter told me that NAL no longer requires agriculture in the educational backgrounds of their librarians. They cannot find librarians with agricultural backgrounds.

Agricultural libraries are not the only ones that cannot find librarians with related backgrounds to fill vacant positions. Libraries cannot find enough catalogers to fill vacant positions, especially if they want foreign language or special subject skills. Schools and public libraries cannot find librarians with backgrounds in teaching or children's literature to fill vacant positions in children's work.

I cannot quite shake the feeling that we are missing the boat here somewhere, and we may be missing it in a great many places.

Recruitment of students to particular disciplines depends on images of the jobs that await them at the end of a course of study. Why are botany and agriculture majors not being recruited to librarianship? Why are undergraduate science majors, education majors, language majors, and majors in other fields where library vacancies go begging not being recruited to librarianship? Instead, career counselors report they see very little professional recruiting at the career fairs they attend. Perhaps an inadvertent result is reinforcement of the stereotype that only people who like books should think about librarianship. That could explain why the stereotypical librarian is, like me, an English major. One more piece of information confirms that undergraduate students are inadequately recruited to librarianship: Few library school students report deciding to become librarians while they were undergraduates.[2]

Our problem is one of image and visibility, going back to the undergraduate experience, and probably even farther, to high school days, as Liz Futas said.

Yet, to be prudent, library schools need to recruit where their investments of time, effort, and money have the best chance of producing students. Library school recruiters tend to be limited to their immediate geographic locations and the population with the greatest interest, namely, library support staff. What we overlook is the recruiting job that could be done by librarians who serve in colleges or departments of engineering, agriculture, education, etc. Librarians can build themselves into an army of recruiters, reaching out to undergraduate career centers in small universities and colleges, participating in career fairs, talking to career counselors, placement officers, academic advisers, and other guidance personnel. Only we can explain that we are not looking solely for English majors, but also for math majors, biology majors, linguists, teachers--in fact, for people from every discipline who are outstanding in academics, who are communicative, and who seem bound for success.

Counselors cannot help but be affected by their perceptions of the careers available and the characteristics they believe necessary to succeed in them. When I visited Montana State's Career Services Office on campus to explain the shortages I had--and, by the way, I was the first librarian to do this--the first words out of their mouths were "You're looking for English majors, right?" Eventually, they sent over to us half a dozen undergraduates. They were chiefly older, female, English majors--but, one step at a time.

---

[2]According to the LISSADA survey, fewer than 17% of the students polled decided to become librarians during their undergraduate careers. William E. Moen, "Library and Information Science Student Attitudes, Demographics, and Aspirations Survey: Who We Are and Why We Are Here, " in *Librarians for the New Millennium,* ed. by Kathleen M. Heim (Chicago: American Library Association, 1988), p. 91-109.

In December and January 1989, with the help and hard work of two support staff members, we filled the display cases in the library lobby with job advertisements, using the tag line, "Who can be a librarian?" Under headings naming fields with large numbers of majors on our campus, we placed job advertisements looking for librarians with those backgrounds, and displayed the list of accredited library programs, along with my name and telephone number. Both reference and circulation reported quite a few nibbles, and I did have one student come to my office. In addition, the two staff members who helped me with the display told their husbands that when they graduate this summer, they need to find jobs where there are library schools.

My talking about librarian shortages to faculty advisers resulted in one student coming to my office and expressing a strong interest in technical services. She had a work study allotment, so we hired her on the spot. She is a business major. I told the agronomy major who maintained the library's plants about the NAL and the Horticultural Librarian advertisements. After she graduated in December, she headed for California with the intention of going to library school.

A picture has emerged in all these discussions about librarianship with students, career counselors, and faculty. Our problem is not necessarily a negative image, it is no image at all. I cannot count the number of times people have said, "I had no idea..." They had no idea there is a shortage of librarians; no idea people with science backgrounds can become librarians; no idea how one becomes a librarian; and they certainly have no idea catalogers exist.

For some colleagues, there are those who believe foreign languages are more important than subject expertise. For me, a dissertation in physics or mathematics, genetics, or ichthyology might as well be in Tamil. Yet I and my fellow English majors are indexing that information for the national database. How many times have you heard, "If you can find me a cataloger with the languages, we can teach him/her enough of the sciences to get by."

We need to do more than get by. We must find ways to recruit in places we have not recruited before. We need to recruit people we have not thought likely candidates to increase not only our numbers, but our variety.

In the meantime, we are not going to turn away those thirty-five-year-old women with their B.A.s in English. Some of us make damn good librarians.

THOMAS W. LEONHARDT, Dean of Libraries, University of the Pacific.

In a study done many years ago looking for the ideal library school student,[3] six attributes were identified that you might not associate with catalogers at all:

- Liking people
- Judgment and an open mind
- Professional responsibility
- Intellectual capacity and interest
- Confidence and animation
- Homely virtues.

I want to dispel the notion that these attributes are foreign to catalogers or not needed for cataloging work.

Also, I am not concerned about whether the current shortage of catalogers is real. Some people say there is no shortage of nurses; just a shortage of nurses who are willing to work as nurses. We have to keep in mind that whether there is a shortage of catalogers or not is beside the point. The point is getting our fair share of the librarians willing to work as librarians.

In many places, particularly in large academic libraries, the productivity mentality is such that librarians in the catalog department are relegated to cataloging eight hours a day, or something approaching that. Catalogers who take off a day to attend a symposium such as this one would be expected to work on Saturday to make up for their lost productivity. This is a counterproductive mentality, and we have to revise that thinking.

---

[3] Ernest J. Reece, *The Task and Training of Librarians* (New York: King's Crown Press, 1949).

When we begin recruiting librarians at any level, I believe we have to recognize that cataloging is a professional responsibility and an activity based on intellectual skills. Theoretical education and keen curiosity about knowledge and its organization are more important than what the cataloger's undergraduate major was.

Administrators and department heads also need to recognize that catalogers are not unsuited for work with the public. Unless they choose to hire such people to fill their cataloging vacancies, catalogers are not misfits; they are not recluses; nor are they detail-oriented compulsives who cannot see the forest for the trees. These kinds of people do work in catalog departments, but they also work in reference departments and in administrative positions. If that is the image of catalogers, or if a supervisor is so intent on getting rid of a backlog that catalogers are cut out of all other normal library activities, then good people will be lost, because good people cannot function that way.

When we look for catalogers, some of the other attributes we seek include higher than average emotional stability, physical fitness, patience, perseverence, and graciousness. We want someone with energy, enthusiasm, and industry. These are the attributes Professor Reece decided were good for recruiting students into library school. My point is that they also are good for recruiting catalogers. We should not recruit catalogers as catalogers, but as well-rounded librarians. Nowhere is it written that catalogers cannot work with the public. That mistaken attitude must be discarded.

I would say that a case can be made for recruiting library school students for entry-level cataloging jobs who have no pre-professional cataloging experience at all, except what they receive in the normal course of the curriculum and, perhaps, some laboratory experience with bibliographic databases. If they are the best and the brightest in their classes, they will become good librarians no matter what specialty we hire them to do. Finding the best qualified person is more than just matching them with a suitable background and experience. Since we are hiring people into a whole work context, we have to look at their whole Curriculum Vitae, their whole background. We are hiring a whole person, a whole librarian, and not just a cataloger.

Let me give an example, if Carol F. will forgive me: Carol F. is at the Massachusetts Institute of Technology now, as Head of Technical Services, but she started out as a cataloger at Stanford. Between these two jobs, however, there was an important step: Carol was hired to be Head of Acquisitions at Stanford even though she did not have acquisitions experience. Had that experience been a requirement for the position, Stanford might have lost a very fine acquisitions head, and Carol's career might have taken a different path. Incidentally, acquisitions librarians, like catalogers, are an endangered species, and as a library director, I tell you much of the blame can be laid at the feet of library directors.

If library school students have undergraduate degrees in biology and master's degrees in library science, they ought to be able to be good reference librarians or catalogers in the field of biology, without advanced subject degrees. They should not need a master's or Ph.D. in a subject field to do a good job. What they need is intellectual curiosity and the capacity to keep up their knowledge, to keep on with their education.

Hiring officers should be looking for the very best person they can find. I know one young librarian who was recruited to be the head of a state university copy cataloging unit, even though he did not have any cataloging background. That upset some people at his university. It upset some colleagues of mine who had worked with him at other places. "He cannot do a good job, because he never cataloged," they said. But, this man's unit doubled its productivity in a year's time. I spoke with his supervisor about it, since the man had worked with me. The man had good managerial skills, a sense of humor, and he got along well with people. He was very bright and learned quickly. He took criticism well. He got the job and is sparkling in it. I suspect such dramatic results would not have been achieved if the institution had selected someone with lots of cataloging expertise, but who lacked the other skills needed to motivate the copy cataloging group to become more productive and, at the same time, to build their morale.

When you recruit new librarians to your library at any level, they will sense the atmosphere in the catalog department. They will sense how catalogers are perceived by the library administration, by non-technical services staff, and by the catalogers themselves. They will see how catalogers are treated. Reference librarians know in advance how many hours they are scheduled for the desk and often can decide whether they want more or fewer desk hours. Reference librarians have other duties, too, e.g., database searching, book selection, etc., and during the hours they are off the desk, they can exercise their judgment about how to carry out those duties. No one counts how many books they select, or judges whether those were good or bad selections. With catalog departments, someone counts how many books each person catalogs, how many books the section catalogs, how many mistakes there were, who made them, and so on. The differences are obvious.

At my former institution, the University of Oregon, we made a concerted effort to get catalogers involved in all library activities. They were offered opportunities to serve on committees, to take on administrative assignments such as acting section head, etc., and given chances to blossom as leaders. When a library does this, offers the same opportunities for promotion and professional growth to catalogers as to reference librarians, cataloging recruits see it. It is easier to recruit the very good person with high aspirations who wants to ensure he or she is not seen solely as a production worker.

We do not need fewer catalogers, we need more of them. Library directors must understand that with our adoption of copy cataloging and new online catalogs, our catalogers should be free to start customizing the local catalogs in ways that reference librarians have demanded for years. This is our opportunity to give really fine public service with new kinds of cataloging, and we need the best kinds of catalogers to do it.

JAMES G. NEAL, Director of University Libraries, Indiana University.

Libraries are faced with extraordinary and unprecedented challenges in managing shifting staff relationships and roles. One area ripe for opportunities for creative change is the traditional division in our libraries between public and technical services. This questioning of our long-standing administrative structures is being fueled by serious difficulties in the recruitment and retention of staff in all categories, but, in particular, professional catalogers. It also is supported by important organizational changes spawned by automation.

My thesis has three elements: First, the division of libraries into technical and public services increasingly is unnecessary and counterproductive; second, original cataloging is carried out most effectively in the context of a broader professional assignment that also involves collection development and direct service responsibilities; third, the distribution of the professional aspects of technical operations produces important benefits for the individual employee, for the library, and for the patron. I hope that patrons are the individuals we will keep in mind.

I maintain that my ideas are supported by trends in three areas: work force development, the impact of automation on personnel, and quality of work life issues. We are faced with unprecedented work force trends, affecting our ability to produce, recruit, and retain quality staff. One contributing factor is that our library schools are producing half as many graduates as they did ten years ago. But it is not the only factor.

My research into professional staff turnover documented low levels of staff movement in academic libraries. A study of 98 of the 106 members of the Association of Research Libraries in 1984, 1985, and 1986, showed a turnover rate of 7.4 percent. A colleague of mine, Richard Rubin, confirmed that the figure for public library staff is very similar for the same period, i.e., 7.5 percent.[4]

---

[4]Richard Rubin, "Employee Turnover among Full-time Public Librarians." *Library Quarterly* 59 (Jan. 1989):27-46

How does this compare with benchmark statistics for other professionals and other groups of employees around the country? Figure 4 shows that the turnover in professional library staff in the United States is very, very low compared to other groups.

My study also looked at why the turnover was taking place, and among which people, in terms of their years of service and their location within the library. For the 1,656 professionals who left their positions in the three year period, the primary reason was to find positions in other libraries and the second most important reason was retirement (see Figure 5). Only six percent of these individuals left to move into other occupations and professions. I suspect that when we collect data for 1987, 1988, and 1989, which we are preparing to do in 1990, that figure will go up significantly. The average length of service for the group as a whole was 8.5 years.

A key finding in the study was significantly higher rates of turnover among reference librarians. The majority of these people were moving to other library positions or to another profession. Catalogers exhibited among the lowest rates of turnover, and the largest proportion of catalogers leaving their positions were retiring. This series of symptoms in work force development, in my view, requires very creative healing.

The impact of automation on workflow and staffing in libraries is producing important changes. The responsibilities and roles of librarians within the library and the communities they serve are changing dramatically. Computerized technology has made possible fundamental changes in the way work is organized and staff is used, with continuing pressures to control costs and improve services. There is a progression as a library goes through the stages of automation from, first, using the technology to do familiar and traditional things faster; next, beginning to apply it to new things; and, eventually, seeking ways for automation to help create changes in the fundamental operation and nature of our organizations. Going from the second stage to the third encourages us to question traditional structures and staff assignments.

Computerizing the catalog has brought about a generalized distributed access to its information. Bibliographic information is available instantly to use when needed, and it is updated directly as new information is added. Among the results of this state of affairs is that understanding of the bibliographic record no longer is solely the province of technical services staff. We are looking toward the successful integration of the gateway function in the online catalog. Bibliographic decisions and processing priorities can be made in the context of the collections and services of which they will be part.

Effective implementation of automation must respond to three employee expectations: The need to understand, predict, and control what goes on in their work environments; the need to experience meaning and purpose in their daily activities; and the need for a moderate degree of variety and change. Satisfaction of these needs can contribute positively to the degree of productivity achieved.

At my former institution, Penn State, we faced difficulties filling a growing number of cataloging vacancies, and we felt we were missing opportunities to increase services. We decided to meet the challenge with a new strategy, and took cataloging out of the dedicated central facility. Cataloging at Penn State now is performed by librarians trained in cataloging, but assigned to public service units, where they serve as subject specialists doing collection development and giving direct service to patrons as well. The automated system at Penn State facilitated this distribution of cataloging work by allowing librarians to focus on intellecutal, rather than formatting, decisions. Public service areas gained staff skilled in the use of the system, who have a formal role in cataloging policy making and priority setting, and who can become the focus for further extension of distributed processing activities. Cataloging staff have first-hand knowledge of collections and user needs, enabling them to be more effective decision makers.

As a result of this organizational change, Penn State is implementing online information systems that are more responsive to users' needs and, at the same time, offering a more exciting and

FIGURE 4

BENCHMARK STATISTICS

(crude separation rates)

professional & technical workers	13%
clerical workers	18%
white collar workers	19%
manufacturing industries	54%
mining industries	38%
communication industries	22%
service organizations	21%
government organizations	23%

FIGURE 5

**ARL UNIVERSITY LIBRARY
PROFESSIONAL TURNOVER**

REASONS FOR LEAVING	No.	%
Retirement	371	22.4
Retrenchment/layoffs	13	0.8
Dismissal for performance	40	2.4
Denial of tenure	23	1.4
Other occupation/profession	99	6.0
Return to school	47	2.8
Family left area	164	9.9
Position in another library	696	42.0
Death	34	2.1
Child-rearing responsibilities	43	2.6
Medical/psychological disability	9	0.5
Don't know/None of the above	117	7.1
TOTAL	1,656	100%

challenging work environment for catalogers. This was not a textbook approach to the relationship between public and technical services. Conditions at Penn State were such that we needed people to fill our vacancies, and our automated system was at the stage where it could support distributed cataloging activity. We had an open, team approach in planning these changes, which gave librarians control over their environment. I think this has been a very exciting experience at Penn State, and our goal continues to be improving service programs in the highly competitive electronic marketplace.

MARION T. REID, Interim Director of Libraries, California State University, San Marcos.

Louisiana State University Libraries, where I was serving as Associate Director for Technical Services in March 1989, has had to plan and strategize creatively to recruit cataloging librarians for some years, since we were unable to fill our vacancies easily. At the time of the symposium, we had three openings. Although Louisiana State University does have a library school, an accreditation team that visited in 1974 said we had too many librarians on staff educated here and that we must hire from the outside. We still are working under that stricture. Jim Matarazzo's statistics told us that only 30 percent of the people who graduate from library schools want to relocate, and the LISSADA study found that only 7.6 percent of the people in library school are interested first in cataloging. That means for every 100 people out there who are getting master's degrees this spring, I can only hope to attract 2.28 of them to come and talk to me about working at Lousiana State (7.6 x 30 x 100 = 2.28). We had, and we have, a problem.

We sat down and really tried to develop an action plan. We had already gone through a search for a serials cataloger, and came up with an empty candidate pool. We tried to add staff temporarily to help the catalogers, because what we are talking about is having half our original cataloging positions vacant. This was successful in part, since one person who had retired was hired back on a half-time basis, another who was working part-time agreed to work five additional hours in cataloging, and a third person, an experienced librarian married to a visiting professor, walked in just when she was needed most and agreed to work three-quarter time. But these are stop-gap measures. We had to do more, to sit down and try to identify potential applicants methodically.

We began by trying to identify former Louisiana State graduate assistants who had worked in cataloging during their library school careers and who were still in the Baton Rouge area, but we didn't find any. We decided to work harder with the placement services that were available to us. Last fall, when I attended the Southeastern Library Association meeting, I went through their job bank, found four possible applicants, and wrote to each one. No response whatsoever. In January 1989, at the American Library Association midwinter conference, our head of cataloging talked with seven people in placement. We were astonished and pleased that seven people actually wanted to talk with us! They all applied. For the set of interviews that we just completed at the end of February and the beginning of March, we had the best pool we have had in twenty years. We had twelve viable applicants and interviewed five: One from another library at Louisiana State; one from Berkeley; one from Pittsburgh; one from Illinois; and one from Chapel Hill. One person withdrew to take an automation position. We made four offers. The person from Louisiana State chose to stay put, not to enter a tenure-track, public-or-perish situation. One person became head of a copy cataloging unit in a southeastern institution, while another decided to go to an eastern school to be assistant head of serials. One offer is still outstanding. Louisiana State still has three positions open, with the possibility of filling one. My colleagues will be visiting library schools for quite a while to come.

We decided to talk with students in library schools throughout the United States whenever we got close to one. When our serials services librarian, a recent graduate of Chapel Hill, visited that campus last October, she talked with people to find out who might be interested in a cataloging position. When I went to a meeting at Stanford, I stopped at Berkeley first, and made arrangements to talk with any current student who might possibly consider leaving the San Francisco area--two people. In November, our director went to Michigan to give a speech, and talked with two people there. This morning, at Simmons College, I spoke to Sheila Intner's cataloging class before they took an examination. I have talked since then with one person and hope to see another person tomorrow.

The bottom line is that we are in a proactive stance, and we must be proactive, because there is a limited pool of people who are willing to relocate and who are interested in cataloging. We must start talking with students while they are in library school, perhaps when they walk into the doors of library schools. This is a competitive situation. We must listen to what the applicants want and we must be prepared to broaden our offers. We are looking for more than "just catalogers".

EDITOR'S NOTE: Each session of formal presentations was followed by free-for-all discussion among symposium participants, with additional questions and comments from members of the audience of about 100 persons. These discussions have been organized around their main themes, not the chronological order in which comments were made. We did this to facilitate understanding of what was said about each theme in its entirety before moving to a new idea. Some speakers were not identifiable from the recorded proceedings; therefore, we opted to omit identifying any of the individual speakers. Instead, we ask readers to keep in mind that the following is a distillation of many comments from various speakers, not a narrative written solely by the editors.

Karen Muller, Executive Director of the American Library Association's Association for Library Collections and Technical Services and Library Administration and Management Association divisions, moderated the first discussion. It is entirely due to Karen's ability to move things along that so much was able to be included here, since only a trifle more than thirty minutes was available before the close of the session.

DISCUSSION #1
RECRUITING CATALOGING
LIBRARIANS

Theme 1: Special recruiting problems for institutions lacking a nearby library school.

There are quite a lot of places in the United States in which there is no friendly local library school--not only in the immediate community, but anywhere in the state or the region. A dilemma surfaces when one ponders the implications of the findings of studies reported in this session, namely, that people do not leave home to go to library school, and once they do go to library school, they are reluctant to leave that area to work: If you encourage your most promising staff to go to library school, you have lost them.

Marion Reid pointed out that for some institutions, at least, even when you have a local library school, you are not without your problems. At Louisiana State and institutions in a similar situation, if you encourage your most promising undergraduate students or your best staff members to attend your local library school, they will have to cease working for you when they receive their degrees.

Some of the schools that closed recently, such as the University of Denver, left those in their local areas without any library school. And, while the output of those schools was small and probably is not much of a factor contributing to the shortage of catalogers, I think the message of closing library schools is very important as well as the denial of library education in that geographic area.

What shall those of us do who work in places like Bozeman, Montana or Boulder, Colorado? If we encourage our staff to go to library school, they have to leave the state and we cannot expect them to come back again. We are going to have to go a little farther in our recruitment efforts than to tell our colleagues to seek out those whom they already touch. It is rather nice to have a personal involvement and influence on people, and it is wonderful to be able to identify terrific staff and put them into the profession. But one has to feel fairly noble to say I would rather have these people enter the field of librarianship than stay here and do my work.

I would like to encourage people who work in academic libraries whose campuses do not have library schools to consider the undergraduate internship as a recruiting tool. I have never considered our undergraduate interns at Brooklyn College as recruits, but, in effect, they are. Many departments on campus allow seniors to earn three credits, the same as for a typical course, for doing special projects. This semester in the library we have seven interns. One of them is from a neighboring library school, but the other six are undergraduates. Two are graduating seniors in computer information science, one in art, two from the English department, and one from the history department. The ones from English and history are working on collection assessment projects. The two people from computer science are working with our systems group in the library, as is the person from the art department, who is doing a lot of work in our Macintosh laboratory. We know that the person from the library school will become a librarian. From our conversations, I think it is very likely that two of the other people will consider librarianship, too. So, although I had not thought of them as a recruiting tool, undergraduate internships seem to work very well.

Another option is for libraries and universities in a region to develop library-based courses and, perhaps, to bring faculty from distant library schools to teach in their local areas. Naturally, courses such as those given in Bozeman would have to be acceptable to library school faculties, to people in the profession, and to the Committee on Accreditation.

Theme 2: Distance education as a solution to the lack of local library schools.

Clearly, the distribution of professional education around the United States is not equitable. It may be possible to redistribute library education in the next decade by means of innovative applications of technology that bring library schools' curricula to locations beyond the library schools' commuting areas. Distance education facilitated by satellite communications and cable television networking is being explored by a group within the Association for Library and Information Science Education, as well as by educational institutions in the larger higher education community. Their success could bring library school classes to Bozeman, Boulder, or anywhere.

Distance learning was mentioned specifically as a way to build up enrollment for a school by a recently interviewed candidate for Provost/Chief Economic Officer at our state university. This person mentioned library science as a problem and a distance learning program as a potential solution. Distance learning could be a way to recruit and teach all types of librarians, and to take advantage of all the library schools with which one has connections. Any faculty member teaching a course in one school could be teaching it to students all over the country, with two-way audio or two-way audiovisual hook-ups.

Distance learning could overcome difficulties that librarianship has, particularly, as a female-dominated profession. Women working as paraprofessionals who might like to get their library degrees may have no options now other than to leave their children to go to a distant library school or give up a job that may be helping a child go through college so that mom can go instead. If women could work toward a degree through television, they could do both at once.

Two precautions should be considered regarding distance education: Teaching in a pedagogically sound manner, and the loss of personal contact. If we rely on technology alone, even two-way interactive video, and do not ensure that this teaching is truly equivalent to the traditional classroom experience, we will only dilute the profession. In the end that could be worse than no teaching at all. And, a great deal is conveyed through teacher-student contact, e.g., acculturation to the profession, discussions of ethics and other ideas that may not be part of any syllabus, but that come up in informal conversations and non-classroom interactions. A real teacher is a role model, by his or her own example, and that is difficult to convey through a television screen. Remote access to a teacher alone is not enough. We will have to tinker with distance education, possibly with some on-site contacts, until we are satisfied it achieves what we do now in the classroom.

There is no question that moving people around physically once or twice a week is a hardship, whether it is getting the students to the library school from a distance, or sending the faculty members out to teach in extension programs. Some measure of relief can be gained by using people from the region to teach in that region's extension program. Often there are expert practitioners who are able and willing to teach. In the University of Rhode Island's experience with extension programming, it has been about half and half, i.e., half local experts acting as adjunct faculty, and half our regular faculty members conducting classes.

Theme 3: Recruiting catalogers with differing backgrounds.

Distance education is not necessarily the way to broaden the backgrounds and expertise of people who go into cataloging. Having that kind of access for the vanilla-flavored staff member working in our cataloging departments now--that is, the thirty-five-year-old, white, female, humanities major--is not going to get us science people, younger or older people, male librarians, black people, native Americans, or any other kind of broadening of the people entering the profession.

Theme 4: All librarians do not agree there is a shortage of cataloging librarians.

We have not convinced our reference colleagues that there really is a shortage. Many of them have been in large candidate pools of vanilla-flavored reference librarians without a second master's degree and without a science background, and, yet, we hire them. They cannot see any shortage. They have just had to compete with thirty other reference librarians and do not realize that, in the cataloging area, we might have had a pool of two potential catalogers, one of whom takes a job elsewhere while we are still in the search process.

I think we need to achieve consensus first that this is an issue. I have heard speakers say there is a real shortage and I have heard speakers say there is not. Either we are right or we are wrong about the shortage. If we cannot even agree on whether or not we need more people within this specialty--never mind how to educate them--how can we begin to solve the problem? We don't even know basic numbers. I think that is the first issue.

I believe we have good evidence that there is at least some kind of a shortage. Look at all of the vacancies that people cannot fill to their satisfaction, even to their moderate satisfaction.

Catalogers are out there, but they are not willing to work as catalogers for any number of reasons. Educating more of them to follow this path is not necessarily the solution.

Theme 5: Bibliographic instruction as a method of attracting undergraduates to library science as a career.

Bibliographic instruction is a way in which librarians reach thousands of undergraduates, and could provide a vehicle for recruitment to the profession. There has been a great deal of talk about the invisibility of library schools on their campuses, yet virtually every student on those campuses receives bibliographic instruction from librarians. Good instruction could begin to get people interested, particularly those who do not want to go for Ph.D.s in a field, but might not want to be bench chemists, for example, after they receive bachelor's degrees in chemistry and find that is the only work they can get. We can begin to strategize from the point where we know we can reach people--and we reach them with bibliographic instruction.

Theme 6: Investing dollars in recruiting to library schools.

One of the volunteer activities some of us do is to recruit for our undergraduate schools at local college nights. The colleges provide some training, usually given by their office of admission's field representatives, and they supply fancy brochures, illustrated bulletins, and even videotapes to support alumni recruiting efforts. Small private colleges are faced with a declining pool of applicants, so they are recruiting and marketing, spending about $1,000 per student, according to some reports. My graduate library school has never asked me to do any recruiting, and I have never heard of anyone else being asked by their library school to do it. And, outside of their bulletins, which are usually very nice, I am not aware of library schools producing recruiting materials that approach those of undergraduate colleges.

Theme 7: Value of the working experience as a recruitment tool.

Something I never regarded as a recruitment tool until I changed jobs is the pleasantness (or lack of it) of the work experience in technical services. During the interview for my new job, I told the library director that technical services was a pit, and it truly is. Whitney Coe talked about the reverse visit, i.e., inviting people in to see your technical services in operation, and I thought to myself, good heavens! If I invited anybody into my technical services area, they would definitely not want to work in technical services. We have mismatched furniture being used for purposes other than those for which it was designed; it has never been below 80 degrees Farenheit in my office; and I could go on. That is something for library administrators to look at, as well. It is not just the content of the job, but the way in which you are allowed to do your job that can work for or against recruitment for cataloging positions.

Theme 8: Lengthening the master's degree program.

The bibliographic record is central to every function in the library and the potential for innovation as a result of advancing technology and new ways to organize information has added so much to cataloging that we cannot teach it all in a one-year program. Because we try to teach everything in so little time, we sacrifice a lot and teach it in a boring way. I find few catalogers with even the vaguest understanding of basic concepts of the relationships of cataloging to other areas of service, yet this is the most exciting and wonderful part of cataloging.

From my experience as a public librarian and also at OCLC, I can tell you it is not enough to get someone coming in who has years of professional schooling and no practical experience. I meet people who know how OCLC terminals function, but have no experience using them. That is not going to get them a job with my organization. But how can people afford a two-year program? It now costs $10,000. to get a $17,000.-$20,000.-a-year job. You do not have to be too bright to figure out the cost-benefit ratio there.

Theme 9: Restructuring technical services to employ librarians to do both cataloging and public service work.

I was interested in what Jim Neal had to say about conditions at Penn State. I am interesting in restructuring technical services and the library generally. I am very much in favor of that, but I have been discouraged because it seems that the whole weight of western history moves toward the division of labor. And it looks as if the computer is accelerating that phenomenon. Perhaps the outlook for a holistic reorganization is more hopeful than I would have expected.

The 1986 RTSD study showed that 65 percent of the job advertisements included some other responsibilities than cataloging. That indicates a trend in that direction.[1] I think the core condition is, however, that you must have a fully developed computerized bibliographic system that can support doing cataloging work in a distributed fashion. Also, we can expect cost analyses will be done

---

[1] American Library Association, Resources and Technical Services Division, Cataloging and Classification Section, Task Force on Education and Recruitment for Cataloging, "CCS Task Force on Education and Recruitment for Cataloging Report, June 1986," *RTSD Newsletter* 11, no. 7:71-78.

and will appear in the literature when these reorganizations have progressed far enough. There was one done at Northwestern University by Karen Horny not too long ago and this year [i.e., 1989] another was published from Penn State. We are just beginning to get some articles written by librarians working at places where there is a track record--where they are not assessing the immediate impact of automation, but the impact once things settle in.

Management structures in all kinds of public service institutions, not just libraries, are going through fundamental changes. Libraries tend to lag a bit behind some of the other types of institutions. It is twenty years since some major corporations and public service agencies have changed their structure and orientation, so I think we are on the brink of realizing more change.

Theme 10: Accepting undergraduate library degrees.

In the United Kingdom, we have a 39 percent decline in applications to all the library schools in colleges and universities last year, and we can guess it is going to continue happening this year, too. In 1990, we have a massive demographic downturn of eighteen-year-olds because of the successful contraception of the early 1970s. So all of the library schools in the UK are terrified at the moment that there will not be any customers in the nineties. Frankly, I do not understand this elitist craziness that you have in the United States that says you must have a master's degree to practice this profession. I cannot understand this absolute obsession with the master's level qualification. At my institution in my school, we have an undergraduate program for a degree in communication studies. We have 2,000 applicants for 28 places, and that is with the demographic downturn. I cannot understand why you do not have an undergraduate degree in information studies, or librarianship and information studies, or make it really sexy and have communication and information studies, which will bring you thousands of students.

You need to look at the way you market the subject. Some people talked about that, but there is a great deal more scope for radically re-examining your higher education as far as the library profession is concerned.

PART II

EDUCATING CATALOGING LIBRARIANS

The session keynote speaker for the Symposium's second session, which focused on educating cataloging librarians, was Dr. Jane B. Robbins, director of the School of Library and Information Studies at University of Wisconsin-Madison. Dr. Robbins served her peers as president of the Association for Library and Information Science Education in 1984, and, always in touch with the world of practice, she also was elected president of the Wisconsin Library Association in 1986 and was named Wisconsin Librarian of the Year in 1988. Dr. Robbins chairs the Standards Revision Subcommittee of the American Library Association's Committee on Accreditation, a body charged with changing the measures and procedures by which programs preparing new librarians are accredited.

Research is an important priority of Dr. Robbins' personal agenda, and she received research awards from the U.S. Department of Education to study libraries' role in alleviating adult illiteracy. Her article, "Yes, Virginia, You Can Require an Accredited Master's Degree for That Job," Library Journal 11 4 (Feb.1, 1990):40-44, earned her a cover photograph, evidence of the importance of library education in the world of practice.

FICTION AND REALITY IN EDUCATING CATALOGERS

JANE B. ROBBINS

Socrates never went to neighborhood block parties, or cocktail parties, or rode on the airlines and so he never had to face a problem common to library educators. You simply cannot introduce yourself at parties or to your seatmate on a plane as a university professor, and certainly not as a cataloging professor. It is like introducing yourself as an alchemist. People do not know what to do with it. They are stranded in a conversational desert, from which they typically try to get out through some kind of tautology, "You teach cataloging?" or some non sequitur. Yesterday, on my way from the airport, the cab driver and I talked about the weather a bit. Then, he asked whether I was here on business and when I said yes, he asked what my business was. I replied, "I teach people to become librarians."

"Sounds dull," he said.

So I said, "I imagine driving a cab is kind of dull, too."

He snickered, and we had a lovely conversation about how dull a lot of work is. Lawyers, can you imagine how dull it must be after a few years to be a lawyer? Writing all those wills! Even soap opera stars probably have very dull lives. They have to spend a lot of time just standing around. And I got to thinking about it. I don't think there is anything dull about cataloging at all. Certainly, it is not any more dull than anything else. The next time somebody suggests it, I think you should go right back at them and suggest that their work is dull. Perhaps it will work.

It is because nobody has any kind of association with a countervailing experience that they can jump to the conclusion that libraries are dull or librarians are dull. As you know, we do not have a great many people out there using the institution. And, they see catalogers, as was mentioned earlier, as far removed from any lively activity.

We are not going to clear up the image of librarianship for people, although I must admit that I really believe that, if the American Library Association and some of the other professional associations in the information area would come together and put together a series of fifteen to thirty market-tested spots on television about interesting young people in the information service industries, I think we could start recruiting people into the field by the dozens. Trying to do it at high school workshops and career fairs is not going to get the kind of splash we need.

After people are enticed into the field, one of the things we know is that within our schools people are stereotyped, too. Once, I heard a couple of students say, "Well, real people go into public services. The people who are stereotyped as librarians go into cataloging."

I thought, "These are people who have just gotten here!"

Stereotyping starts from the very beginning and I am not quite sure where it comes from. Perhaps certain of our faculty members contribute to the process. I have heard more complaints about negative stereotyping of children's services librarians than catalogers. But, those overtones are in our schools, having their effect on students from the very beginning. Providing students with some countervailing evidence that it is not true is an important thing for us to do.

On the other hand, one of the questions I asked myself when I started to work on this presentation was whether any hard evidence supported the fact that people think this way. My wise old mother once said to me, "You know, Jane, the problem with stereotypes is that there is evidence out there to support them." One also must take into account that the stereotype makes seeing people who fit it stand out. Can you see me recruiting people to the faculty saying, "You don't look like a cataloger, so we are going to have you teach cataloging in order to provide a countervailing piece of evidence that may help get our students to study cataloging."

I looked in the literature and found one study done in 1980 by Suzanne Frankie, who is the University Librarian at Oakland University at Rochester, Michigan.[1] Dr. Frankie's doctoral dissertation provides us with a piece of pretty good empirical research; but, since it is only one piece and very little has been built upon it, I am going to ask you to disregard it after I tell you about it.

---

[1] Suzanne O. Frankie, "Occupational Characteristics of University Librarianship," in *Options for the '80's: Proceedings of the Second National Conference of the Association of College and Research Libraries, Minneapolis,* edited by M.D. Kathman and V.F. Massman (Greenwich, Conn.: JAI Press, 1982)

Remember, we cannot do very much with just one piece of research, no matter how good it is, and I do not want you to think it is true just because I repeat it. If we do not have more research confirming what Dr. Frankie found, we cannot assume it is true.

Dr. Frankie decided she did not like the image of librarians, and she was tired of hearing people talk about the difference between catalogers and public services people, and she was going to put an end to this once and for all. She did a survey of catalog and reference librarians employed in sixteen large university libraries. Her final sample included ninety-nine cataloging librarians and ninety-four reference librarians. She gave them certain standardized tests and looked at them first as a group of librarians against a norm group of several different types of professions. Then, she looked at the difference between the catalogers and the reference people. Dr. Frankie found that, yes, unfortunately, librarians are very different--a statistically significant difference--from the norm group of eight populations in other professions.[2] The other thing she found out is that there is, indeed, a statistically significant difference between people in cataloging departments and reference departments, so that we do have two subgroups of workers employed in these sixteen large university libraries.[3]

Having told you this, I am going to disregard it and assume that this does not hold true universally, since I cannot talk about improving the teaching of cataloging if I think that the problem is catalogers.

One way to solve the problem of how many people become catalogers is to make the teaching of cataloging really neat. I find it difficult to believe that we cannot communicate to our students that bibliographic organization is the one piece of intellectual property that belongs to us and nobody else. Nobody in any other area of any university claims bibliographic organization for their discipline.

---

[2] Ibid., p. 409.
[3] Ibid.

Management of information services and delivery of information services are claimed by other departments, even though that is our work, too; but not bibliographic organization. It is the heart of what we do; it is what everything else we do is built upon. And cataloging is the star within that particular group of subjects. How can we fail to see it as the exciting thing we all know it can be?

Maybe what we need is better teaching of cataloging. To begin, let us look at where cataloging teachers are coming from. Last year, eighty-two people received doctorates in the field of library and information studies. Over half of those people were not interested in education for librarianship. They got their degrees for other reasons. A dozen more (sometimes this group can be as many as twenty, depending on the year) were non-U.S. international students who went back to their own countries. That left around twenty people who were looking for jobs in library education. At the January 1989 annual meeting of the Association for Library and Information Science Education in Washington, there were fifty-four faculty openings in schools of library and information studies, of which a large portion were in the area of bibliographic organization.

What happens--speaking from my experience as the administrator of a library school--is that I say to myself, "Oh, boy! What am I going to do?" and I start to look around for practicing catalogers to do some of this teaching. Now, accomplishing this is not easy, either. First of all, universities feel very strongly about the educational preparation of people who are teaching, especially in a graduate program. Adequate preparation to them means having a Ph.D. in your subject. Secondly, catalogers are all so busy. You haven't enough people working for you, as the recruitment presenters told us. Imagine Marion Reid, with three people missing from her catalog department, running over to LSU's library school to teach cataloging, which, you know if you have done it, is not an easy thing to do. One does not just run in and discuss cataloging with a group of students for a while. Teaching requires a great deal of thinking, structure, and preparation--and excellent teaching requires much more time and energy. Teaching is an amazingly intensive job.

If we want to engage people in cataloging through excellent teaching, turning to people in practice who are willing to spare a few hours a week is not the answer, although I am sure some people working in the ranks of cataloging departments also could be gifted teachers. Which brings me to another issue that has occupied my thoughts, lately: It appears to me that, in addition to having a shortage of professional catalogers, the catalogers we do have are spending more and more of their time training support staff people to do what they just learned how to do in library school, because the nature of the work is changing. Teaching of cataloging is going on in the library's cataloging department instead of in the library school. Without getting into it too deeply, this worries me, because such training tends to be solely for the job at hand as opposed to encompassing some larger sense of education about where that job fits into the overall delivery of information services.

It occurred to me that just as we might have some national television spots to improve our image, perhaps we should have some national courses available for the education of support staff people in technical services. These could be delivered through an organization such as the Association for College and Research Libraries, which offers various continuing education courses. At the very least, it would relieve the people who are running cataloging departments from some of the burden of educating and training support staff. Or, we could use distance education to teach cataloging to support staff. At Wisconsin, we have been teaching off-campus for many years and we have some evidence that the people are learning. We taught cataloging in the extension program last fall and did a lot of testing to compare whether those students could pass the same tests our students on campus took. There was absolutely no difference between them. In fact, in this particular test, the off-campus people outperformed the campus-based students. Test them again and scores might flip the other way, but, at least, we found out that they are learning.

Perhaps the cataloger shortage is caused partly by what professional catalogers are being used to do. The cost in time and money of having individuals teach cataloging to support staff again and again in individual libraries builds quickly. Some of the dollars that are going toward keeping that up could go to support a national training program, maybe using distance learning techniques, to take this off the backs of individuals and to get more effective learning for their dollars. The shortage might dissipate to some degree if we did that.

One thing of which I am sure is that really good teaching cannot hurt as we try to entice people into cataloging. I also am convinced that not-so-good teachers can be taught to teach better. They might not become great teachers, but they could do better. We know some things about good teaching. We know it needs to be vivid, memorable, relevant, and clear. We want to teach people not only what it is like to catalog, but what it is like to be a cataloger. Our students want desperately to know what the job is going to be like. What is the Gestalt? We should be able to showcase cataloging as one of the careers that people choose. A sense of humor is one of the essentials of good teaching, too. Some of the teaching of cataloging I have seen has been so frantic about getting everything covered that there is no room for humor. Cataloging can be very funny. There is a woman in Au Claire, Wisconsin who keeps a list of funny LC subject headings. I got hold of her list and provided it to our cataloging teacher, who made it a staple of the class. I just love REFUSE AND REFUSE DISPOSAL--RELIGIOUS ASPECTS!

Some people think that if students are having a good time, they probably are not learning anything, but there is abolutely no evidence to support that at all. Students remember the things they laugh about and it need not disrupt the flow of learning.

Now, I shall let others take off from here, hoping that I have succeeded in dispelling some treasured, but mistaken, notions about education for cataloging.

Seven speakers followed keynoter Robbins. All but one, Joseph R. Matthews, Vice-president and General Manager of GEAC International, a computer company, were library school professors, having direct knowledge of the problems of teaching cataloging. In this session, certain themes presented in the recruiting session emerged once again, including the changing nature of cataloging work and the need to give students portable skills. Here, however, speakers also explore d the changing character of library and information science students, the specifics of cataloging work, and methods of introducing students to the complex web of standards require d for understanding the bibliographic universe. The range of solutions offered by the speakers in this session cover a wide territory, yet none appear particularly difficult to implement. The remarks that follow seem appropriate not only to the university setting, but, with some adjustments, they can apply to the library setting as well.

THE EDUCATION OF CATALOGING LIBRARIANS

MICHAEL CARPENTER, Assistant Professor, School of Library and Information Science, Louisiana State University, Baton Rouge.

Several things have changed since Panizzi's time, in the mid-nineteenth century, when he called the teaching of cataloging "a narrow, rugged, uninteresting path" that demanded from its students "a patience and labor which few will deem well bestowed."[1] First of all, the students of cataloging I will talk about are enrolled in graduate programs in universities, not learning on the job. Second,

---

[1] Sir Anthony Panizzi, "Mr. Panizzi to the Right Hon. the Earl of Ellesmere.-- British Museum, January 29, 1848," in "Commissioners Appointed to Inquire in the Constitution and Government of the British Museum," *Appendix to the Report of the Commissioners Appointed to Inquire into the Constitution and Management [sic] of the British Museum* (London: 1850), p. 378-95.

students are older than they used to be, averaging in their thirties, according to the statistics of the Association for Library and Information Science Education.[2] Third, the practice of librarianship is changing so that the requirement that every librarian be able to catalog his or her collections is giving way to the recognition that many, if not most, of the students in our core cataloging courses will never have to catalog anything. How might these three factors alter our perceptions of what is appropriate content for the first cataloging course, that is often required of all students?

Panizzi knew what he was talking about regarding the drudgery of data input. It drove his staff members to drink, and some drank on the job, forcing Panizzi to go to the trustees and have them thrown out of the library. But cataloging does not consist only of data input. Rote learning does not belong in a program of graduate study in a university. Teaching cataloging as rote learning seems inappropriate in library school classrooms. I suggest it is a wrong-headed approach.

Adult learning at the graduate level ought to focus on the attributes of mature adults. Undergraduates, who are in the early stages of cognitive and ethical development, typically take the party line straight from faculty members. If library school students start off immediately after completing their undergraduate careers, they are probably in the same mold, willing to take the party line, whatever the professor--representing authority--has to say. But the more mature students we are encountering these days do not take kindly to that sort of teaching. Thirty-five-year-olds readily question authority, and they want to think things through on their own. It is time for them to develop their own critical thinking and all we professors can do is encourage them in the endeavor. Laying down the law of *AACR2* does not mesh very well with that. Quite the contrary. It helps us make cataloging appear to be a dull subject,

---

[2] Association for Library and Information Science Education, *Library and Information Science Education Statistical Report* (State College, Penn.: the Association, 1983-1987).

maybe even driving them to drink. Only, unlike Panizzi, we do not have trustees to back us up and throw them out.

We would do better to teach our students how to analyze the rules, how to find out what is wrong with them, what could be improved, to synthesize, to learn how to examine a bibliographic control system and arrive at a new one, especially in our changing library environment. Finally, and most important, we should teach them to evaluate cataloging systems. Which ones are good, and why? Which are bad, and why? Mature graduate students are ready to learn cataloging values, such as not misrepresenting the facts, being accurate, providing a serviceable catalog intelligible to users. These are the kinds of issues mature students are ready to tackle and will not think dull.

What do we traditionally try to do in our cataloging courses? We aim for the ability to apply a known set of rules. We aim to turn out someone who can provide a little bit of Dewey, a little bit of Sears. In other words, we are trying to turn out someone who can step into their first job and catalog. We have to acknowledge that one course in cataloging cannot do this. Students who are going to go out and catalog will have to take advanced courses to teach them the nitty gritty of rules and tools, and after they are hired, they will need on-the-job-training to complete their education.

The learning of cataloging does not have to be dull and the responsibility for not being dull rests squarely on the shoulders of the professor. I believe a good approach is not to teach a course in data entry, but to teach what might be called cataloging appreciation, appreciation of the values of cataloging. I admit this sounds much like music appreciation, which my junior high school daughter once called "clapping for credit." But, we have to face up to our objectives here. Do we want to train catalogers in the first course, or do we want to get the students who are good to go into the practice of cataloging? I think we want the latter course. The library school core course is merely the entry into cataloging. We need to get our students to appreciate cataloging, not to get drunk on the job.

Lubetzky's notions that the professional school should teach people to be more than practitioners, to teach them also to be thinkers and critics,[3] is what I would like to advocate as the one main objective our core cataloging courses should undertake to accomplish.

CAROLYN O. FROST, Professor and Assistant Dean, School of Information and Library Studies, University of Michigan, Ann Arbor.

A survey of 182 University of Michigan library school students, conducted during the fall of 1988, demonstrated that very few (2 percent) chose cataloging as their first career choice, but nearly one-third were favorably disposed toward positions having some cataloging duties, and nearly three-quarters believed that cataloging required problem solving and analytical abilities, and that it involved decision making and judgment. The survey also revealed that the strongest influence on students' career choices were work experiences and contacts with practicing librarians. Only about one-third of the respondents said that they were influenced by courses or by professors.

Some of the conventional wisdom was upheld by this small survey, i.e., that very few library school students opt to become catalogers; but, some of its most negative aspects were denied, e.g., that cataloging does not employ analytical skills, or that catalogers do not have to use judgment, solve problems, or make decisions. Most of the students surveyed did not agree with the negative stereotype of the cataloger, although nearly half of the respondents believed that cataloging work was repetitive and routine.[4]

---

[3] Seymour Lubetzky, "On Teaching Cataloging," *Journal of Education for Librarianship* 5 (Spring 1958), p. 257.

[4] Details of the findings are elaborated in Carolyn O. Frost, "Preaching to the Unconverted: The Cataloging Educator's Challenge," in *Recruiting, Educating, and Training Cataloging Librarians: Solving the Problems,* edited by Sheila S. Intner and Janet Swan Hill (Westport, Conn.: Greenwood Press, 1989), p. 187-195.

What are the implications of these findings for librarians? It seems likely that a fertile area for recruitment lies in the library work environment. Librarians appear to be in a key position to influence paraprofessional staff to consider cataloging as a career. Further analysis of the survey data by type of library experience reveals that students with work experience in cataloging departments were much more likely to regard cataloging as a career choice than were students with other kinds of work experience. I also found that students with reference experience were much more likely to be receptive to the idea of a cataloging position combined with other responsibilities.

This would suggest that library administrators should be encouraged to restructure cataloging work, and to expand the role of catalogers to include a range of activities and responsibilities involving other departments, along the lines indicated by Jim Neal. This would capitalize on the willingness of a large minority of students to engage in some cataloging, if it is not done to the exclusion of all other types of library work.

What are the implications for library educators? If cataloging related courses focus solely on students who already have an interest in cataloging as career, the audience will be very small, indeed. One strategy is to develop broadly-based courses that have relevance for both cataloging and non-cataloging specialists. The reality in my own classes is that I have large enrollments in elective cataloging courses. My last course in cataloging nonbook materials was closed because we reached the limit of forty, and this class was made up mostly of students whose primary interests are in areas such as reference, bibliographic instruction, school libraries, special libraries, etc.

Cataloging professors need to stress the broader application of cataloging skills. We can emphasize the transferability of the skills needed for cataloging, including decision making, problem solving, management, communication, and instruction. For example, *AACR2* is perfect for learning decision making skills. Liz Bishoff and Jane Robbins pointed out that the increased use of paraprofessional staff means that professional catalogers have to become skilled in developing training programs. Communication also is important as integrated library systems bring catalogers in closer working relationships with other departments. Students need to be given opportunities to show how they would communicate their cataloging knowledge to their peers, or to patrons, or people they supervise. In examinations or projects, I ask students to show how they would present what they have learned to someone else in a workshop, a manual, or some other kind of presentation.

Finally, cataloging professors need to include a professional socialization component in their classes. Jane Robbins touched on this. While the image of cataloging is not as negative as some thought, there still is a need to define the cataloger's role more clearly, and to foster the development of a stronger professional image. Cataloging courses can introduce students to professional ethics, issues, and problems as well as providing cataloging content.

In conclusion, few students want to become catalogers, although not from lack of interest in the subject area of cataloging or because of a paucity of available cataloging classes, at least, not at the University of Michigan where there are a number of elective courses with large enrollments. Other factors must be at work. Many students express willingness to include cataloging as a part-time responsibility, even though they show a strong preference for working directly with library patrons.

If these findings are applicable to the larger universe of library school students, then libraries need to develop positions that allow catalogers opportunities to interact with other librarians and with patrons. Particular emphasis should be given to the potential of the paraprofessional work environment, since students' perceptions may be influenced in large measure by their work experiences and their contacts with practicing librarians. Library school cataloging courses must be shaped to attract a broad constituency and must stress the ways in which the cataloger's skills are applicable both to the immediate and the broader work environments.

SUZANNE HILDENBRAND, Associate Professor, School of Information and Library Studies, State University of New York, Buffalo.

Cataloging has its problems, and my thesis is that they occurred because cataloging is one of the most female intensive subsets of the professional of librarianship. Notice that I said female *intensive* and not female *dominant.* The difference is subtle: There are a lot more privates in the army than generals, but who has the dominance and the power in the army? Certainly not the privates. Thus, female intensive professions are those in which most of the practitioners are female. Where the power resides is another issue, and, in the case of cataloging, we do not know.

I believe that four clusters of characteristics need to be investigated to determine whether cataloging is, truly, more female intensive than the rest of librarianship. These four are: (1) the sex ratio in the specialty; (2) the distribution of men and women in cataloging activities; (3) the status, image, and/or the reputation of the activity; and, (4) the conditions under which cataloging librarians do their work. I hypothesize that, in fact, cataloging is more female intensive than librarianship generally and, therefore, each one of these characteristics will show up more negatively than for the profession as a whole. It is as if the problems of librarianship as a whole are writ larger here in cataloging, because it is an even more female intensive activity.

In this presentation, I shall lay out the territory and speculate on what little evidence exists, but I can only speculate. The evidence to uphold or deny my thesis is missing from the literature, and gathering and analyzing it could provide material for several dissertations.

It has been very difficult to gather any kind of statistics in librarianship by sex. Now, after a long and heartrending struggle, we have them by type of library, although not by type of activity. It is not a question of asking people their job titles. We know, and the presentations that preceded me have confirmed, that job titles are getting very murky. The procedure used by Roma Harris at Western Ontario, is more appropriate. Ms. Harris used the percentage of time spent in tasks to measure whether a job falls into a particular category.[5] She did this with graduates of her library school and found out that, indeed, a far higher percentage of women than men were doing cataloging tasks, e.g., assigning subject headings, descriptive cataloging, etc. Harris did another piece of research indicating that cataloging has been a predictably feminine activity in library education.[6] I have to laugh because there are three men and four women among the seven people in this session--not a very good demonstration of female intensive-ness. However, if we discount Joe Matthews, who is not, strictly speaking, an educator, the ratio changes to twice as many women as men.

These few pieces of evidence are suggestive, but not enough to come to firm conclusions about the accuracy of my hypotheses regarding the sex ratio, and they do not address the issue of distribution of men and women within the various subsets of cataloging activities. It remains to be seen whether studies directed specifically at these issues continue to confirm that cataloging is female intensive.

Salaries in the last round of the ALA Salary Survey showed that people called reference librarians were making $500.00 more than people called catalogers at the same institutions. I would point out that this is actually a worse deficit than it seems if you recall that the survey includes catalogers at academic libraries who often are required to have one or two foreign languages and some other fairly exotic skills. Cross-tabulating the salary deficit with the level of

---

[5] Roma M. Harris, Susan Monk, and Jill T. Austin, "MLS Graduates Survey: Sex Differences in Prestige and Salary Found," *Canadian Library Journal* 43 (June 1986), p. 151.

[6] ------, B. Gilliam Michell, and Carol Conley, "The Gender Gap in Library Education," *Journal of Education for Library and Information Science* 25 (Winter 1985), p. 167-76.

required skills, years of service, etc., might show an even more important discrepancy.

A key study in assessing the status, image, and reputation of cataloging activities is Ruth Hafter's, reported in *Academic Librarians and Cataloging Networks*. [7] Hafter comes down pretty negatively on catalogers and cataloging. She conducted a series of interviews and learned that not only was this view shared by many of the academic library administrators she interviewed, it was shared also by the catalogers themselves.

Regarding working conditions, many people in the audience know about these problems better than I do. Someone in the Recruiting session spoke about mismatched furniture and unpleasantly high temperatures. Every time I go into the cataloging department at one major university I am struck by its similarity to the old time typing pools in the insurance companies. It is a big open area with all these people at their desks filing cards and papers. I think it is significant that only two people in this large department have offices they can go into and close a door to have privacy. Only two people have their own telephone line. We call this professional work and these people have to face a tenure review for which they must do research and publish, yet they cannot get away from the buzz of the corral. How can they possibly accomplish their academic requirements with no privacy, no telephone at their desks, etc.?

What happens is that the library is so desperate to retain their catalogers that they are not held to the tenure requirements. I suppose the library director pleads that they cannot be denied reappointment since it is so difficult to hire good catalogers and train them. Such actions breed a bad attitude toward catalogers. Others claim that, although catalogers may have faculty status, they do not deserve it and they really do not do any research and writing, similar to the requirements the rest of the faculty must meet.

---

[7] Ruth Hafter, *Academic Librarians and Cataloging Networks: Visibility, Quality Control, and Professional Status* (Westport, Conn.: Greenwood Press, 1986).

In addition to the physical environment, another aspect of working conditions is career development. At my university, we had an incredible case where, because of the shortage of catalogers, people working in that specialty were denied the right to apply for a splendid career development opportunity offered in the State University of New York system. They were told at the institutional level they could not apply, because the library could not afford to lose their services for the period of time it took for the training.

I seem to be coming down on the side of working conditions that are a big turnoff to our students, contrary to what Carolyn Frost just said. Clearly, we need to determine whether what I describe is as prevalent as I believe it is, or whether she is correct and my few observations are anomalies. Furthermore, even if I am correct, does it do any good saying that this is attributable to the fact that cataloging is more female intensive than the rest of librarianship? Some of my friends have said, "Oh, so the answer is fire all the women catalogers, right?"

Clearly, that is not the answer, but the knowledge that it is true (if, indeed, it is) gives one a certain leverage. If you can identify an area where working conditions are worse and the only difference between it and other areas in the library is that more of the people in that area are female, then you have, in fact, a sex equity issue. You have a lever. That lever can be used to rectify the situation, to improve working conditions, or, better yet, to restructure the work and distribute the jobs more equitably. Get some private offices and telephones on their desks for those cataloging librarians who are supposed to make professional judgments and think critically. How can they think at all with telephones ringing and people running around and book carts going by?

Libraries are desperate for catalogers, but it is very difficult to attract library educators' attention and to get them to acknowledge that it is important. There are similarities between the unresponsive attitude of schools of education toward teacher education and that of schools of library and information science toward cataloging education. My hypothesis is that, in both instances, the underlying reasons need to be examined carefully in terms of gender.

SHEILA S. INTNER, Professor, Graduate School of Library and Information Science, Simmons College, Boston, Massachusetts.

Six developments in the information world beg for responses in cataloging education--the educational process that is primarily aimed at preparing librarians to organize information successfully. The first is an increasing complexity in the nature of information products that forces cataloging to be more sophisticated. Libraries used to collect books, each containing a single work written by one author. A book tended to focus on a single subject that, in Cutter's time, could be represented by one subject heading, could be assigned a simple classification number, and could be placed on a shelf with other books on that subject. Disciplines were clear-cut in their objects of study. Chemists studied chemistry and historians studied history, and the two were very unlikely to meet in the same book. Today we deal with multi-authored, multi-disciplinary works. Depending on the problem, a large research project might be conducted by a team consisting of scientists from different specialities, an engineer or two, an economist, and a sociologist. The results of their research may appear in a videorecording, a magnetic tape reel designed to be mounted on a computer system, or a multimedia package. Dense media such as serials and microforms typically are issued with many works in one physical unit. Cataloging this material and deciding how best to make it accessible to those who wish to use it is a challenge of no small proportions.

The second development is a proliferation of diverse groups of information consumers. The image of information consumers as a homogeneous group of people sharing a common language and common purposes has given way, at least in the North America, to a plethora of information-consuming groups, each with different characteristics in background culture, intellectual skills, and educational levels as well as in their reasons for seeking information. Scholars and lay searchers alike are being sensitized to new data sources with large potential, e.g., computer-based networks, fax machines, and other new technologies.

Third, new technologies for input and communication of bibliographic information are causing a fundamental shift in the way this information is created, manipulated, displayed, and used. Today's computerized environment requires knowledge of and commitment to national and international standards. It requires understanding of computing and its many subfields: database design, screen display, hardware, software, system architecture, networking, etc. It requires that our vision of bibliographic control be revised in terms of new capabilities, dramatically different from the capabilities of the card files being replaced.

Fourth, the rules of cataloging, subject headings, and classification are evolving more rapidly than they did in the past, in response to the changes described above. It is not easy and can be unsatisfying to operate in an environment in which standards seem always to be in a state of flux, where work done today may be obsolete tomorrow. It is frightening and frustrating, and demands that catalogers accept a heavy dose of ambiguity in their work.

Fifth, the rise of computerized shared cataloging networks has caused the division of labor in cataloging departments to change, and added managerial duties to the job descriptions of many, if not most, cataloging librarians. The presence of bibliographic networks containing millions of catalog records enables staff with different education and training than that of cataloging librarians to handle a substantial proportion of the cataloging work. Instead of spending the bulk of work time cataloging new materials, the cataloging librarian is expected to recruit and train paraprofessional staff, plan personnel deployment and workflow procedures, and worry about budgets for the department and its systems, and to catalog "as time allows."

The sixth development in the information environment is that cataloging systems are no longer contained within the cataloging department. Isolation of cataloging from other library service centers has ended with the deployment of terminals carrying bibliographic data into every library department. Librarians in other service centers realize they have a major stake in the catalog, and exert their influence over it. At the same time, catalogers are being asked to apply their expertise in non-cataloging areas for the librarians outside cataloging departments. Some catalogers may shout "Hooray!" for this, but others are profoundly disturbed to be exposed to the criticism of non-cataloging colleagues and to spend time on their problems.

The two responses I propose are a teaching method that emphasizes decision-making based on information research and analysis (SERA: Stimulation, Experimentation, Resolution, and Analysis), and a larger curriculum in the beginning, or core cataloging course that introduces all the elements that make up a cataloging career (WYTIWYG: What You Teach Is What You Get).[8] How do these proposals address the issues of change?

SERA teaches a process for finding answers to difficult questions. It does not arm the student with a lot of answers that they can apply to whatever comes across their desks. Even the answers (read, *rules*) we have now are flexible and require judgment. This causes great discomfort among some of my practitioner colleagues, who prefer being given one right answer over making decisions and interpreting principles on their own. SERA also draws the student into active participation in the learning process. I agree with Michael Carpenter that this is absolutely essential in dealing with adult learners, and it foreshadows their obligation to continue learning after they leave library school.

---

[8] Sheila S. Intner, "Responding to Change: New Goals and Strategies for Core Cataloging Courses," in *Recruiting, Educating, and Training Cataloging Librarians,* p. 227-43.

Once, a cataloger I chided on not keeping up with the literature wrote me a lengthy letter complaining about his long hours and many obligations, explaining how hard it was to keep up with the many changes in rules and developments in automated cataloging systems. I wrote back, asking: "Would you have your appendix removed by a surgeon who had not kept up with the field since receiving a medical degree in the 1960s? Would you allow that person to practice on you?" The cataloger wrote back, replying, "It is not the same." Well, I am sorry, but it is. Librarians take on an obligation to keep up with their field, or they become like the surgeon who has not read in the medical literature since graduating from medical school. You do not want that surgeon cutting you open. And you do not want that kind of librarian filling your information needs.

SERA furnishes flexibility of two kinds: training for facing the new cataloging problems one always will encounter; and experience in seeking alternative solutions, having tradeoffs of various kinds, instead of just one right answer. SERA emphasizes the dynamic nature of decision making and its dependence on information, analysis, and interpretation.

WYTIWYG acknowledges the changes in cataloging librarians' job descriptions and the importance of the conglomeration of new bibliographic structures we call "the national database." WYTIWYG does not simplify; it attempts to identify the parts of mainstream bibliographic control systems we encounter now. WYTIWYG includes an introduction to electronic standards, networking, managerial issues, etc., in addition to the elements of cataloging and classification we always have taught. It introduces noncataloging librarians to the components of bibliographic control, an understanding of which is essential for everyone who deals with bibliographic systems, whether to prepare data for input, to decide methods for sorting, storing, or retrieving data in the system, to interface the system with other systems, or to use the system to find answers for patron questions.

Although it is tough enough to teach what is now crammed into core cataloging courses, we need to teach an even larger curriculum. We need to reach both Carolyn Frost's seven percent who wish to be catalogers and the ninety-three percent who do not. The large group of librarians who do not learn more about bibliographic control or get involved with cataloging and classification also need this knowledge. As public service librarians, they will use bibliographic systems in many ways for patrons; as administrators, they will make decisions affecting the shape and disposition of bibliographic systems. In any roles, librarians need to be aware of the overall structures, underlying principles, and processes at work in the bibliographic universe.

BEATRICE KOVACS, Assistant Professor, Department of Library Science and Educational Technology, University of North Carolina, Greensboro.

The University of North Carolina at Greensboro has an ALA-accredited library science program, but we are one of five departments in the School of Education, instead of being a school ourselves. We share all the resources of our school with four other departments, including pedagogical studies, curriculum and supervision, counseling and counselor research, etc. The battle for the dollar is intense. Thus, even though we have a student body that ranges between 70 and 80 full time equivalents, we have only five full time faculty and a limited budget for adjunct faculty and visiting instructors. As a result, we have only one course in cataloging. It is a required course, very basic, that, in the three credit hours or forty-five contact hours, must cover description and access, subject cataloging, classification, MARC records, and a little bit about international aspects.

The class includes students who wish to study cataloging and classification in depth, and are frustrated by their inability to do so in one three hour course. The class also includes students who have no interest whatsoever (as far as they know) in cataloging and classification, but who are there because it is a required course for the MLS degree. The course must be designed to provide an optimum learning situation for both extremes and for all the people in between. Each semester, the class is composed of people without any library experience, or with very little library experience, plus a few who are currently working in a technical services department, perhaps even as copy catalogers; it also might include a professional librarian or two coming back to update their knowledge. Our solution to the problem of presenting the widest range of information possible in a severely limited time frame is to provide a microcomputer-based study module for students to complete outside of class. If a student wishes, the study module can be enlarged beyond the exercises required for class; and, if not, it provides exposure to real world problems involved in acquiring and using vendor-developed, as opposed to cataloger-developed, computer systems for cataloging.

We developed a microcomputer cataloging laboratory, funded primarily through grants from a variety of sources including the university, the State Library of North Carolina, and some software producers. We obtained a corner to plug in our equipment and store the software in one of the university's academic computing satellite facilities located next to the library science classrooms. (The satellite facility is moving to a new building, leaving us to find new space--space with adequate security, electrical connections, etc.--for the microcomputer cataloging laboratory.) Laboratory assistant Beth Reichardt assists students working through the programs and answers their questions. The study module consists of a two and one-half hour OCLC tutorial demonstrating the MARC standard, and an evaluation of IBM- and/or Apple-based stand-alone cataloging software, most of which does not meet the MARC standard.

During the 1987-88 academic year, student reactions to the study module were very positive. Because of the compressed timeframe, however, summer session students could not use the equipment and software one-on-one with the laboratory assistant. Instead, they had to be satisfied with a forty-five minute version of the OCLC tutorial Beth presented in class, and a demonstration of each type of stand-alone software. After the classroom demonstrations, students had to input one record using one of each type of program.

Microcomputer cataloging laboratory exercises supply many learning experiences. First, they give students hands-on experience with computing for cataloging. For some students, this is their first opportunity to do any sort of computing and they are able to put their fears about that to rest. Second, students make connections between the abstract "rules" taught in the classroom and practical applications in computer systems currently being sold to librarians in the field. They see what is good and not-so-good about different types of hardware, operating systems, and applications packages. Some students believed the computer would "do it all" for them. With these exercises, they find out very quickly that it does not. The terminology learned in the classroom is reinforced as students work their way through inputting records into the databases. The time and practice spent on inputting exercises helps students develop stronger foundations, especially in descriptive cataloging.

Students find that concessions must be made in order to use the commercially-marketed cataloging software. We try to guide them to make assessments of the concessions in terms of meeting the information needs of users the system will serve. Even after graduation, some students ask to come back to try some of the other programs they know we have and to obtain additional practice using them.

Any agency in the community that wishes to come in to the laboratory to work with any of the cataloging programs can make an appointment to do so. Either the laboratory assistant or I take them through the programs. This service is especially helpful for agencies that do not have libraries, but want to organize materials in-house. As word spreads about the availability of the laboratory, we are receiving more inquiries. We believe the laboratory could also be used to help practicing librarians update their knowledge.

The principal drawback to the microcomputer study module is scheduling, both for the students and for the laboratory assistant. Originally, we envisioned a self-study laboratory where students could use the equipment and software on their own to learn what the programs could do, aided by the manuals. We soon discovered that most of the manuals we have are not adequate for this purpose, and the valuable assistance provided by the laboratory assistant was essential to successful learning experiences. Although the laboratory assistant has flexible hours, matching students' schedules with hers sometimes is impossible. Many of the students commute long distances and work at full time jobs. They are able to be on campus only a few hours a week, mostly in the evening, so the logistics get a little complicated.

Nevertheless, we are encouraged by responses to a survey of student attitudes toward the microcomputer laboratory study module. Fifty-four students currently involved in the cataloging course responded to the survey, and all either agreed or strongly agreed that the module was helpful, useful, enlightening, and educational. They all disagreed or strongly disagreed that the module was unnecessary or confusing. When asked for their perceptions of the advantages of software for catalog record production, comments included the following: Programs save time, are easy to use, add punctuation, standardize catalog records, are labor-saving, cost-effective, efficient, are flexible, can be done on-site, and that they save typing card sets or waiting for card sets. One person said that the programs are fun to use. Asked to comment on the disadvantages of the programs, students said: Programs may not meet the needs of a specific library; one needs to understand the quirks of a system; software and hardware are costly; and one may have fear of computers or fear of power failures. Thirty-five of the respondents could not think of any disadvantages. Finally, asked to specify what they learned from the module, students commented that they learned such programs existed, they had hands-on experience using them, each system has good and bad features, system options vary, not all programs conform to cataloging rules, and that programs are easy to learn, teach, and use. Two people learned that the perfect cataloging program is waiting to be written.

The fifty-four people surveyed included forty working in libraries, ten of them in technical services. Four students reported seeking cataloging as a career path (7.4 percent).

At the beginning of the course, students are warned they will not become expert catalogers, or even experienced catalogers by the end of the semester. They are told they will have a foundation in the language and concepts of cataloging and classification that could open up an entry level career path, if they choose to take it. But, even if they choose not to become cataloging librarians, the knowledge they acquire will be helpful in providing an awareness of the complexities of organizing collections for future decision making in public services, administration, and other aspects of librarianship and information service.

JOSEPH R. MATTHEWS, Vice President and General Manager, GEAC Computers International, Markham, Ontario.

As a high school student, I cataloged three-fourths of my high school library's collection in an after-hours exercise. I learned by necessity and by trial and error about things such as authority control, vocabulary control, and control of classification and Cutter numbers. The experience is one I recall generally with fond memories, one that makes me identify with practicing catalogers, despite my ignorance at the time of rules and tools. Unfortunately, all of my cataloging still is in use at that high school.

Since I consider myself part of the cataloging profession, although it is without the official sanction of a library degree, I hope you will permit me to point out that, generally, in our discussions of cataloging and technical services, we fail to place a four letter word in our foundation: User. Never has a profession been indicted by its clients as has the library profession. All one needs to do to see it is to read the catalog use studies and look at the failure rates of card catalog users. It is absolutely embarrassing, yet the cataloging profession continues to focus on other issues, the wrong issues, in my view. Catalogers focus on the minutiae, on the elementary things they say cause problems in the catalog. While observations on the minutiae are interesting, they are not where we should focus our attention to do something about our abysmal track record of user search failure.

When I was in graduate school, I was a research assistant. My professor said, "I hate to use the library, Joe, and your job, since you are my research assistant, is going to the library for me."

Being a dumb graduate student, I asked, "Why can't you go? Why do I have to go?"

And he replied, "There are a few things about the library I just can't cope with on an emotional level, like the card catalog. Therefore, you are going to go for me."

I would go over to the library with a huge list of materials to retrieve out of the collection for the professor. I would go to the card catalog and try to go through it systematically, and I would experience a typical failure rate. Depending on the type of search, I would succeed half the time, or a third of the time, and I would get very frustrated. So I developed a coping mechanism. I lied. Instead of searching the card catalog myself, I would go up to the reference librarian and say, "Gosh, I looked in the card catalog, but I am having trouble finding these materials. Could you be of assistance?"

I also learned which were the good reference librarians. Some would never leave the desk. They would just extend their index fingers and say, "This book is over there; this book is over here," etc. I call that the "pointing approach" to reference service.

The helpful reference librarians would accompany me to the card catalog and we would start going through my list. They would fail to find the first item on the list and I would say, "That is too bad."

And they would reply, "Now, we must be persistent," and I would agree that we must.

We would try different access points each time we failed to find something. After a while, we would work our way through the list and find most of the materials the professor wanted. But, it was too much for me, a poor user, to cope with alone. The only way I could manage was to lie and say, "Yes, I have tried," and obtain the expert assistance of the librarian. Most patrons do not do that.

We should ask the question, "What is cataloging for?" And, embedded on every page of every cataloging text, should be that four-letter word, "User." We are here to serve our clients, yet, when I served as a liaison to a committee at the American Library Association for two years, the Committee on Cataloging: Description and Access, I sat at the end of the table and listened to countless discussions of minutiae until, at the end of the day, I would raise my hand and ask, "What does this have to do with access for users?"

After a while, the other committee members would look at me and say, "Okay, Joe, it is time for your question," because that was the only thing with which I was concerned.

Cataloging classes I have observed are immersed in identifying the trees rather than the forest with which we must deal. There seems to be much talk about access, with little recognition of who that access is intended to serve. I believe automation offers a number of ways to help teach catalogers and cataloging, provided we first change our focus and, as our foundation, identify where we are going and why we are going that way. If we can agree that user service is catalog's fundamental aim, then we can employ computers to deal with the minutiae and allow catalogers the luxury of thinking about the user.

Computers can automatically move students or novice catalogers through the cataloging process, furnishing the necessary information as they go. The MARC format template can be programmed into the computer so that automatic prompts present catalogers with a list of valid choices, e.g., for the appropriate format, content designation codes, and punctuation. Cataloging rules and rule interpretations can be displayed as needed. After the data is input, running a spellchecker could reveal spelling and typographical errors. Without much effort, the computer also could check and supply conventional abbreviations for publishing houses and their locations, illustrative material, edition statements, etc. Headings in newly-entered records could be matched against online name and subject authorities, so that unauthorized words, including errors, would print out for authorization or correction.

For catalogs as well as computers, consistency is paramount. My friend Larry Osborne, Associate Professor at the University of Hawaii, tells students that it is more important to be consistent than to be correct. As an automation consultant and a computer vendor, I agree. I worked with one library that put local call number information in a hundred different locations in their MARC records. Developing a computer program to fix that automatically would take a staggering amount of money and time. In the end, it had to be fixed by hand, one record at a time, and it was very expensive. Had the catalogers entered all that data in the wrong place, but done it absolutely consistently, a program could have been written to make corrections with no great effort or cost.

Catalogers might consider a different question: Who may add cross references? One would think the logical folks to add cross references to local authority files are public service librarians, who hear the search words that users have tried without success. A few years ago, a British library did a study in which they took 100 books in each of two subject areas and asked a group of fifty cataloging librarians to catalog this material. When the catalogers were all done creating the catalog records, the library put them into a little online file and asked 100 library users to come in and search the file. The users were asked to choose search terms of their own to find books in these two topical areas. Guess how much overlap there was in assignment of subject terms? The answer is, less than twenty-five percent. This study suggests we need to get smarter in the way we go about assigning subject search terms, especially since vocabulary evolves and changes constantly. It is reference librarians in particular who are on the receiving end of the continuing change; as such, they should be empowered to add cross references.

The first time someone comes in and says, "I want a book about the space shuttle, and I could not find it in the catalog," should be the last. The first time, the librarian takes them over to Big Red (i.e., the three-volume set of *Library of Congress Subject Headings*), and, if it is a good reference librarian, helps them locate the correct subject heading. (If they search Big Red by themselves, it will be sheer luck if they find the authorized heading is "Reusable space vehicle.") The second time a user comes in and says, "I'm interested in the space shuttle, because I've just read an article about it," a link should already have been created between "Space shuttle" and "Reusable space vehicle" in that library's catalog. If not, how many times should the library catalog and Big Red be allowed to fail the user, before you, the librarian, say, "Gosh, maybe we ought to add that cross reference"?

Enormous potential exists for catalogers to use computers to handle the minutiae of cataloging. If computers attended to the details, cataloging productivity would improve and, more importantly, catalogers could turn their attention to the unresolved issues of user access.

FRANCIS MIKSA, Professor, Graduate School of Library and Information Science, University of Texas at Austin.

The Cataloging and Classification Section Task Force study[9] said that cataloging curriculum has been losing out in library schools over the last ten years. In the paper originally prepared for this

---

[9] Janet Swan Hill, "CCS Task Force on Education and Recruitment for Cataloging Report, June 1986," *RTSD Newsletter* 11 (1986):71-78.

symposium,[10] I examined the position of cataloging in library school programs over the last 100 years, the way the Task Force study did it--by looking at the courses called cataloging--and I learned that we started losing out long before the last decade. We began losing out in the 1920s, and in a curious way. When library schools began and started teaching library economy and bibliography not yet organized into a formal curriculum, cataloging was a large part of the program. In the 1920s and later, courses were organized into a two-level curriculum: core courses and electives. Immediately, cataloging, which was a large proportion of the earlier program, became only one of the core courses. If you had four core courses, cataloging would be one of them; if you had five core courses, cataloging would still be just one of them. So we lost out. As for the electives, there would be a couple of advanced courses to represent the advanced features of cataloging.

Over the sixty years from the 1920s to 1980s, we have not done badly in the core. But, in electives, we seem to have lost out terribly. As a proportion of the curriculum, courses called cataloging now are minuscule compared to courses called everything else under the sun.

The conclusion that there is a much smaller proportion of cataloging courses in library school curricula today depends, however, on how one defines cataloging courses. Defined as courses named cataloging, the conclusion is undisputed. But, I found three definitions of cataloging that developed historically. The first definition stresses cataloging as the entire process of making a system of bibliographic entries. It is a Charles Cutter-style view of the whole thing, because he started at a time when there were no catalog systems of any merit. Cutter had to start from scratch. In Cutter's situation, you talk about users, you talk about

---

[10] Francis Miksa, "Cataloging Education in the Library and Information Science Curriculum," in *Recruiting, Educating, and Training Cataloging Librarians,* p. 273-97.

making the system, you plan the system, you design it and implement it, you maintain it, you monitor it, you change it, you adapt it, you supplement it.

The second definition of cataloging perceives cataloging solely as entry preparation. The third definition is cataloging as management of the operation, which, for all practical purposes, means everything except creating the system, because the system is a given.

In the early days of library education at the Columbia School of Library Economy, cataloging lecturers talked about authority control and the objects of the catalog. They did not use those terms, but that is what they meant. Over the next forty years, the triumph of cataloging means that cataloging becomes entry preparation, because the system is a given--you do not have to create it. The Library of Congress (LC) gives you the system and you just prepare entries for it. That seems to have occurred by the 1940s, as far as I can tell. And, another concern came out in the 1930s and 1940s: cataloging as management. When catalogers are let loose to do exactly what they want, they prepare very expensive entries. The library management says, "Hey, you must control costs," and the emphasis in cataloging shifts to technical services management, oriented primarily to controlling costs.

Since information science came into the curriculum, a startling new thing happened. Information science and document retrieval studies are, essentially, system oriented studies. They deal with how you create a document retrieval system by one of several different methods. The whole thrust of technology is to focus on the entire system. If we include in our definition of cataloging courses those courses that deal with setting up document control systems of one sort or another for retrieval, we actually have an expansion in our area, not a decrease. But, it is not called cataloging. It is more generic.

Cutter said that the golden age of cataloging was over. He said it because LC cards came along and they killed it. You did not have to make your own system any more. Making your own system is where the real excitement and intellectual stimulation is. When LC cards came along you did not have to make the system. You could not affect the system. All you could do is input into someone else's system, and that is drudgery.

I think the golden age of cataloging is back. I think it is here again because of our microcomputers, because of our technology. Technology gives us the wherewithal to set up all kinds of alternative systems, not just the one standardized system someone else decides should be there. I did this whole study about meanings to get at a broader definition of cataloging. I do not care if we call it bibliographic control or document retrieval as long as it includes the sense of making a system--not simply preparing entries for it, but making the system itself.

Now, how does this translate in terms of our library school curriculum? We have a core course and we have advanced courses in cataloging. I think that first course ought to be a course in what Michael Carpenter called cataloging appreciation. It is, fundamentally, the ideas about the whole system we want to convey to students, to hook them and get them excited about it. When they are hooked on it, you will have some who want to do it for a career. Those will have to be taken through the nuts and bolts, and it is hard going, because there are so many details in document retrieval systems with which we deal. There are more details in bibliographic control than we will ever find in any other part of our field.

What does cataloging appreciation mean? It means grasping the notion that the idea must come first and the details afterward. A few months ago, we heard an inspirational tape recording during a faculty retreat. Some fellow was talking about curriculum planning and he said that you can do anything you want if you have an idea of it first and that idea drives you. That goes for cataloging, too. I want to share with you a metaphor for the idea that drives me when I teach cataloging to beginners:

This metaphor is a picture of me driving my fast, sleek, brand-new car. I like driving my car, driving it fast, feeling it grip the road, listening to the interaction of all the parts, hearing them working together, making a great-sounding hum. It is not just the car alone, it is me and the car. It responds to me and the directions I give it through the steering wheel, the accelerator, the brakes, and I respond to its sounds and the power I sense coming from it. The car and I become one powerful, fast transportation system that works smoothly and efficiently. When I am using the catalog, searching it, the catalog becomes part of me and I tune myself to it. The catalog is one of the most sophisticated information retrieval instruments ever created by humankind. Card format, machine format, it does not matter. It responds to me and I to it. When the catalog and I are working well together, we become a beautifully tuned system. It is an exciting experience. The catalog and I become a human-artifact response system that is absolutely mind boggling. It gives me a thrill, just as I get a thrill from driving my new car.

A second metaphor I have for cataloging is washing clothes. I was a single parent for a while. Do you know what happens when you are a single male parent? You are raising children, but you never learned how to do the laundry, or, perhaps you never learned how to cook because someone else did it for you. It was scary because there were so many details to learn--the machine and all its dials and settings, the water, the detergent, the bleach, the softeners, and the timing of every part of it. Cooking was just as bad, and I had a terrible time trying to get all the different parts of the meal cooked. Nobody told me what the outcome would be, whether I could get all the dishes on the table together. But we had to eat and we had to have clean clothes. I made some terrible messes, but I had to keep trying and it drove me on. I realized it was all right to to try and make mistakes. I just threw them out, washed them over, or ate them anyway. The challenge was to make it all work, to have a beautiful pile of clean clothes or a great meal on the table. I see that same sort of challenge to my students when they are learning to make a catalog system. They have to have a vision of it in their minds first. It is all right for them to try and to make mistakes, then to see the vision of the catalog system they want to make, and try again. I believe that is cataloging appreciation.

The first cataloging course should help students capture an idea, a beautiful idea, that includes that four letter word of Joe's, the user. The catalog system is not just the catalog by itself. It is a catalog-user system. Making that system, visualizing that system, is what we should cover in our first course.

The discussion following the second session was led by Janet Swan Hill. She began by asking the group to consider a number of provocative questions, including the following: Is the shortage we have identified the result of what we are asking catalogers to do? How can technology help us? Are we treating catalogers as professionals in terms of good working conditions and career development opportunities? What about cataloging education? Are we meeting our library students' learning needs? Have we addressed changes in the profession in our teaching methods? Can we rearrange our educational delivery methods to reach the appropriate people with the appropriate content, and do that economically? Can we define a curriculum for cataloging appreciation? And she added that she liked the last-mentioned idea a great deal. Unfortunately, not all of Ms. Hill's questions were answered in the discussion. She closed the session with an incisive remark made by Charles Cohen, President of the Newbery Library in Chicago, at a luncheon held at that institution on 29 November 1988: "Upon graduation, I realized that I have only learned how to learn."

DISCUSSION #2
EDUCATING CATALOGING LIBRARIANS

Theme 1: Incorporating the notion of "building the system" into cataloging courses.

We talk about the golden age of cataloging returning because we have a chance today to build the whole system. For library school courses to reflect that sense of building a system we need more courses on subject access, particularly relating online bibliographic retrieval to cataloging. It seems that teaching about OCLC and teaching about DIALOG are destined never to meet.

A new program in our school is called Archival Enterprise. It talks about putting archival materials into systems for later retrieval. It does not have much to do with *AACR2* or MARC format, and the archivists, not catalogers, are doing it. Another is records management, where documentalists, not catalogers, talk about organizing records. Who in the library is doing the most creative work in making new systems? It is reference librarians. They are not afraid to put up throwaway systems on a microcomputer-- systems that will be used for six months and then discarded when the need has passed. Catalogers are not involved in these efforts because they are too busy with the "given" system for which students only need to prepare records.

Courses that study local systems and local systems design are taught in many schools. In them, we take the "given" system, the standard cataloging system, and teach students how to manipulate it to provide the kind of access we want in a local system. That is cataloging, too.

We have to be a little more broad-minded about looking at new databases built by technologists. We should be willing to look at which standards can be altered or ignored for the moment to assist in achieving other goals.

No matter what information you want to describe and no matter what kind of file you put the information into, the problem is getting it out for the user. Systems such as OCLC, RLG, and LC's bibliographic control systems were built twenty years ago. Users, librarians, and system designers are all smarter now, nothing has stayed the same. It may be a painful thing to build our bibliographic systems over again, but we have to do it, and, in the future, we will have to do it over again. Each time the system should be better.

Theme 2: The one year master's degree is too brief to teach what needs to be learned.

Most library school master's degree programs last one year. One year is too little to teach students all these wonderful things, including enough knowledge of software so they can help build our bibliographic systems.

In the standard, quick-and-dirty thirty-six hours, how can we fit in the philosophical basis of what it is we do and the factual basis needed to develop the philosophy? In the core cataloging course, I sense a goal ambiguity and an ambiguity related to student characteristics. In one course, we try to create school librarians who can catalog a little, reference librarians who can use catalogs, and real catalogers with full professional powers, all in the same forty-five contact hours. But, we are in a reality where, in many places, we only have one cataloging faculty member.

The way you get people into cataloging is to give them an experience of the work itself. People we attract into cataloging are those who have cataloged, or almost cataloged. We hear people talk about the distinction between education and training, and the necessity of teaching cataloging appreciation and broad conceptual knowledge. But, if you cannot also, in the graduate program, expose people to the actual operation of cataloging, you are not going to attract catalogers. It cannot all be done in a single year.

It is clear that there is no way we can extend the master's degree to two or three years. I am not sure that everyone who works in a library at the professional level has to have had four years of an undergraduate education followed by an additional year or two at the master's level. We could insert some of what we teach into our undergraduate programs and attract good people without undermining the master's degree. Business, social work, and journalism are all professions that have graduate and undergraduate degrees. People study them at the undergraduate level, and some go on to study at the graduate level. Employers know who to hire--they hire people with undergraduate degrees for some jobs and those with master's degrees for other jobs. There is a lot to learn, and all of it does not have to be jammed into the one-year master's degree. Employers, professionals in the field, and the library schools have to get together and say, "Let's do it." The universities will be glad to have us teaching at the undergraduate level. Let us have more library education, but let us build a system that is flexible and realistic. I think putting pressure on the professional associations might produce some good results here.

Theme 3: Catalogers may be losing their hegemony over bibliographic organization.

I am concerned that catalogers are losing ownership of the concept and the delivery of bibliographic organization. I see that the people developing bibliographic systems are not catalogers. They are vendors, writers of software, computer system designers, etc. It is the people I fondly call "techno-twits" who are taking the leadership and the ownership of bibliographic organization.

Coming from "techno-twit-land," I know one of our biggest problems is that the analysts and programmers go to the librarians on our staff and ask, "How do you want this to work?" and rely on their answers. Some of our staff librarians give answers based on how bibliographic systems were used ten years back, when they were working in libraries. They need to know more about the way our systems are used in the library today. Also, use of bibliographic systems is changing rapidly. It is easy for local system vendors to become submerged in the workings of their own system, without regard to how they could or should work in the library. When librarians do not communicate what they need successfully to the programmers, the "technotwits" take over.

If library schools stressed software development as part of regular school programs, it might help catalogers secure "ownership" of bibliographic organization from programmers and software analysts.

Theme 4: Knowledge of use environments and users is a valuable cataloging specialty, too.

Another knowledge area unique to our field is that of information use environments. We know more about them than any other academic discipline. There are some intersecting fields that know a great deal about a very narrow range of use environments, e.g., business scholars know a lot about that special information use environment, but we have the broadest spread of knowledge about use environments of any field. I think it would be appropriate to our curriculum to give intensive exposure to students in how to measure use, how to define it, how to identify user categories, etc.

Fran Miksa said we have a lot of information about users and how they use information. I have to differ with that. With apologies to Joe Matthews and the others who studied catalog use in the Council on Library Resources project,[1] we learned a lot, but one thing we did not learn was how people use information systems. We must start gathering data using unobtrusive methods so we can learn about it, and use it to improve our bibliographic systems.

Theme 5: Educators and pragmatists view cataloging from different perspectives.

Ten years ago, when Fran Miksa was at Louisiana State University, he came to me and asked, "Do your catalogers know how the users are using the catalog? Why do you use this subject heading?"

---

[1] Joseph R. Matthews and Gary Lawrence, "Further Analysis of the CLR Online Catalog Project," *Information Technology and Libraries* 3 (Dec. 1984):354-76.

I thought to myself, "That is not what we are trying to do. We have this system and we are trying to implement it."

What I see here are two different groups. One group, the educators, is talking about developing systems. The other group, the pragmatists, is trying to deal with the existing system. Perhaps we could cross-pollinate somehow. Is it possible to have professors on leave from the educational system come into the pragmatic setting and help us look at the system and discuss ways to change or improve it? It is too much to expect of the people who come out of library school and begin working in the library, because they do not have the scope. Educators must help pragmatists investigate the problems.

Theme 6: Cataloging educators may vary widely in their knowledge and preparation.

It is fine to look at cataloging courses and see what is happening to the teaching of cataloging, but we must also look at who is teaching them. In many schools, I believe, adjuncts teach cataloging. Adjuncts are well prepared to teach entry preparation. They keep up on rule changes; they know about the cataloging systems in use in their libraries and managing the catalog department. But, they may not be as well prepared to discuss the more abstract issues of system design and user-system interaction that Fran Miksa spoke about. In some schools, cataloging is being taught by recycled faculty members who heard there was a shortage of cataloging teachers, so they applied for those positions, even though they had never cataloged. That type of cataloging professor is not able to excite anyone about cataloging.

PART III

TRAINING CATALOGING LIBRARIANS

The keynote speaker for the symposium's third and final session was Henriette D. Avram, Associate Librarian of Congress for Collections Services. Recipient of countless awards and honors, Mrs. Avram is well known as initiator of the MARC format and MARC distribution network. The successes of the national bibliographic network, in which the Library is a leader and major contributor, are the result of her personal vision; its problems have been her concern for more than twenty years.

Mrs. Avram is responsible for the training of more library staff members than any other single individual in the United States. Nearly 1,500 of the Library's staff members work in areas under her leadership. All receive training not only when they begin their careers at the Library, but whenever changes occur in procedures, systems, or in the work itself. To handle this mammoth training task, Mrs. Avram established a central training facility, the Library of Congress Technical Processing and Automation Instruction Office, and she supervises its effort s to supply needed knowledge to librarians working in a most dynamic environment.

The Library of Congress is named many times in the foregoing presentations. Sometimes it is mentioned with gratitude and admiration; at other times its name is pronounced with distress; occasionally, with rancor. Whatever the message, the buck stops at Mrs. Avram's desk. Decisions made and activities taking place at the Library of Congress eventually affect all of the nation's libraries and librarians. So, naturally, it is to the Library of Congress that U.S. librarians look for leadership in solving the problems of training cataloging librarians.

THE FUTURE OF STAFF DEVELOPMENT

HENRIETTE D. AVRAM

Recently, talking to colleagues who are heads of technical processing activities in large research libraries, I hear them say, "We take this record, a copy cataloging record, and we put it in our catalogs no matter what it is like. We have no time to do anything else." As a result, I am interested to hear that participants at this symposium are concerned about a shortage of catalogers. It is not that I have a problem with copy cataloging versus original cataloging. Even we at the Library of Congress would love to begin doing copy cataloging. But, I worry about what is happening. When clients use our catalogs, we know what they retrieve. What we do not know is what they missed. I also worry about the future: What are we doing to the catalogs of the future? There is something of a dichotomy between those of us at this symposium sitting here worrying about the catalog, and some of the directors of large university libraries not worrying about it at all.

When a cataloger arrives at the work site, he or she should be ready for the training in the practices and policies of that particular organization, because he or she understands what we are trying to accomplish. Before he or she comes into the library, education should have provided the knowledge and theory underlying our goals and objectives. The elements of excellence and excitement need to be introduced again into the education of cataloging librarians. Students must be impressed with the knowledge that bibliographic control is fundamental to all library operations, and that point needs to be stressed throughout the curriculum.

We are at a point where the networking infrastructure is such that cataloging data created by professional catalogers is likely to be shared at national and international levels. The sharing is facilitated through a variety of established channels, including uploading to and downloading from bibliographic utilities as well as loading tapes and CD-ROM disks into local systems. Sources for the data being loaded include the Library of Congress MARC Distribution Service, the bibliographic utilities, and commercial vendors. This process will accelerate now that computer-to-computer linking is a reality via the Linked Systems Project.

The primary concern in the profession has been and should continue to be insuring effective and comprehensive bibliographic control. Material that is not accessible is, in effect, useless. Cataloging provides accessibility to material, and the quality of cataloging depends on the knowledge and skills of the people who do it. To be effective, catalogers must be well trained in addition to being well educated. Any investment in their training is an investment in the future enhancement of comprehensive bibliographic control for this country and, indeed, the world.

I must stop for a moment to describe to you my introduction to cataloging. For those who do not know already, I confess I am not a professional librarian. I am what I call a "brainwashed librarian". My introduction to bibliographical knowledge was through a wonderful person at the Library of Congress, Kay Guiles. We had a library card as large as a whole blackboard, and Kay and I went up and down that cataloging entry. We would get to certain places and I would stop and ask, for example, "Why are there parentheses around the series data?"

Kay would think for a while and would say, "Wait here, I am going to find out."

Half an hour later, he would return and say, "Nobody knows any more. But, if we did it, there must have been a good reason."

The training stuck, and, subsequently, former Deputy Librarian of Congress Bill Welsh teased me about it, exclaiming, "There is nothing worse than a convert."

The assumption is made, erroneously, that the advent of automation in libraries has obviated the need for well educated and well trained catalogers. That is not true. Because of automation, it is more important than ever that catalogers be prepared to do high quality work. Automation has provided us with the means to distribute any cataloger's work to libraries around the nation and beyond. Automation has given us the means to manipulate bibliographic data more expediently, but it has not altered the principles of bibliographic control. No matter what format and type of catalog, its function remains the same: To identify uniquely each person or entry, to collocate the works of each, to establish bibliographic relationships as appropriate, to represent each bibliographic item only once, and to show where it is in the particular library's collections.

The use of automation and machine-readable cataloging means the work of individual catalogers is no longer isolated within their libraries and localities. A cataloging record produced at the local level has a strong chance of being contributed to a national file and to an international file as well. Our task, as educators and as work-site trainers is to impress upon catalogers the importance their work is likely to have. Advances in computer-to-computer linking through the Library of Congress's Linked Systems Project (LSP) eventually will allow direct, automatic exchanges of bibliographic records in the future between local library systems and the Library of Congress as well as between computer systems in the United States and those in other countries of the world. Inaccuracies in bibliographic records at local levels will have a strong likelihood of being compounded throughout the world in this growing universal bibliographic network.

At the Library of Congress, cataloging is akin to a scholarly assembly line. The size and complexity of operations within the processing department have made cataloging functions highly specialized and varied, involving three computer systems, seventy languages, and many different material types. Major changes have been occurring with regularity, from the initial implementation of MARC in the 1960s and 1970s to our current experiments with whole book and direct online cataloging. For every change in any part of this vast operation, anywhere from a few dozen to several hundred or more employees require training. This, plus the training of new staff members, adds up to an enormous workload for the Library's Technical Processing and Automation Instruction Office (TPAIO), which I established in 1985 to coordinate and direct training activities. TPAIO's staff of six or seven are the training experts for the department's seventeen divisions, furnishing direct training whenever possible, and coordinating the training done by others when it is not. Having one office coordinate all training efforts promotes consistency throughout the Library. TPAIO supplies a core of expert trainers who are consulted in the early stages of a planned change and who are included among the members of every planning and implementation team.

TPAIO also assists staff members charged with training who are themselves in need of teaching skills by periodically offering a course called "Training the Trainer." A by-product of this course is a manual devoted to training the trainer that can be used by staff as they embark on future training assignments. We are developing a proofreading course to be used in terms of revising cataloging entries, which is a problem at LC. We have another very successful course that I insisted upon giving to all our automation people, including the head of the Automation Systems Office, called "Cataloging Concepts for Noncatalogers." A course called "Bits and Bytes" was designed to teach our librarians the inner makeup of the computer, the hardware and software. We also are doing a great deal of equipment training, e.g., for the use of special terminals for input of Hebrew records into the RLIN system. TPAIO does all kinds of microcomputer training, e.g., in the use of workstations as well as in the use of microcomputer-based software, e.g., statistical programs, word processing, and many more. We are exploring the idea of making these courses available through the Cataloging Distribution Service, if there is an interest in the library community in acquiring them.

I have been asked if LC will train other libraries' catalogers. After all, changes made in our operations often must be adopted by our outside partners, especially by participants in the National Coordinated Cataloging Project. We also recognize that our decisions are adopted by large numbers of libraries that participate in networks requiring it as their bibliographic standard. We can barely keep up with our own training demands, but we would certainly like to share our knowledge and make our courses available, if that will help meet the needs in the field. The first of the courses we are publishing is "Training the Trainer," but others may follow, depending on the demand for them.

The effectiveness of our information systems is due in large measure to the cataloging they incorporate. Training future catalogers will not be a simple task nor can it be accomplished quickly. Production of high quality cataloging will depend on the priorities we assign to the preparation of knowledgeable catalogers, priorities determined both by educators and practicing librarians. Training of cataloging librarians will continue to be the domain of libraries buttressing the education dispensed by the library schools. A situation having the immediacy and the broad concern as does training for cataloging will require a commitment and an outlay of resources commensurate with the need. At the very least, library decision makers must shoulder their responsibilities:

- to acknowledge the importance of the job and its broad impact;
- to realize that training requires special competence and skill;
- to recognize that cataloging training is complicated and takes time;
- to understand that catalog operations are dynamic and changing;
- to prepare for a continuing training component in their institutions.

Four speakers made presentations that differed substantially from their written papers in the third and final session of the symposium,which focused on solutions to the problems of on-the-job training. One of them, Maureen Sullivan, was not in the original group of speakers whose papers were published in Recruiting, Educating, and Training Cataloging Librarians, *thus, her presentation is given here in full. As in the other sessions, the theme of addressing changes caused by computerizing bibliographic data and cataloging operations ran through these presentations. But one cannot lose sight of other problems with which catalogers have had to deal for years, e.g., quality control, finances, administration, etc., also mentioned by one or more of the speakers. Several innovative solutions are suggested here that undoubtedly will benefit fro m experimentation and refinement. It is clear that symposium participants believe training is an integral component of the professional development cycle, together with recruitment and education.*

ON-THE-JOB TRAINING: ISSUES AND ANSWERS

NANCY L. EATON, Dean of Library Services, Iowa State University.

My first boss at the University of Texas at Austin believed that cataloging experience was the best way to start one's career in librarianship, and I concur. My beginning as a cataloger provided the foundation on which I have built my career, first branching out into automation and more recently into still newer areas with the National Agricultural Library text digitizing project. The bibliographic record is the building block for all the systems with which I have worked. In fact, recruiters might interest students in cataloging by showing them what happens to people who start as catalogers. I believe what happened to me is not an isolated example. I suspect if recruiters select a group of young catalogers at random and track their development, they will find an incredible array of fascinating career paths after several years that might not look at all like cataloging.

Training cannot help but be affected by what is happening in the use of electronic systems for cataloging operations and catalog displays. Until a few years ago, computer-based cataloging systems were quite stable. A library joined a bibliographic utility and once catalogers learned that system, operations were documented and became routine. In the very recent past, that stability has been shattered. Local libraries are building and using combinations of national networks with mainframe- or minicomputer-based local systems, and microcomputers, some or all of which may be linked. There are new concepts in which the online catalog is perceived not solely as a local tool or even as a shared union catalog, but as a link extending to other databases. What does it mean for the training of catalogers to realize all of these possibilities simultaneously?

The inner linking of systems in different ways has complicated ordinary cataloging quite a lot. In my own institution, performing ordinary cataloging routines such as searching for cataloging copy, editing and downloading records, ascertaining authoritative headings, etc., might involve four or five different computer systems, each having its own requirements and limitations. Catalogers must learn how to move in and out of those systems, completely apart from knowing the content of cataloging. This argues for catalogers becoming increasingly sophisticated about selection of large and small systems, knowing the features of systems, the implications of using them, and how one melds those systems into a working environment that makes sense. Unfortunately, the larger vision of creating a working environment frequently is lacking, and the library ends up with a broken patchwork that is difficult to use.

One organizational response in libraries is to create a database management unit. Another response is to merge the systems and technical services administrations into one unit, because they have much commonality. Whatever the strategy employed, realization of the implication of cataloging decisions on system use argues for an interdisciplinary approach to bibliographic systems and database management within the library field. The approach may be called interdepartmental planning, integrated planning, or whatever, but it grows out of the fact that a decision made in one part of the library has a major impact on other parts of the library. Training goals also become interdisciplinary when departments interact.

It is common for libraries implementing new systems to put together task forces that cross departmental lines so that decisions are considered and agreed upon by people on the receiving end as well as by those at the input end. The NOTIS system provides good examples, because its database can be designed in different ways. When branch libraries are brought in, NOTIS can merge the records and display them as a single database or keep them distinct as multiple databases, displaying them separately. Decisions to display records in a particular way has a major impact on the way people interpret the data, and the kinds of help they will need. If bibliographic data is not clear and easily understood, there will be a direct impact on the lines at the reference desk. On-the-job training must prepare librarians to address these considerations knowledgeably

A decision to load government documents into the online catalog and have them display along with other records cannot be made lightly, because experience shows that use of documents may go up 200-300%. That kind of impact should be debated with public service people, not made solely from the viewpoint of technical service operations. Loading Center for Research Library (CRL) records into an online catalog presents a different set of problems, since the records represent materials located off campus. High demand for off campus resources may tax the library's ability to handle the requests.

The catalog also may be used for audiovisual materials and museum artifacts. We find ourselves training the audiovisual librarians and museum staff in the use of the realia formats for storage and retrieval of all sorts of nonbook materials. Suddenly, the cataloging department is a resource for the use of MARC records in the management of unfamiliar kinds of databases.

The National Agricultural Library's (NAL) full text project on which I have been working extends the demands made on catalogers. We are experimenting with scanning full text and preparing it for distribution to libraries. Catalogers are not only doing bibliographic descriptions according to OCLC standards, they also are assigning keyword descriptors and providing abstracts. In turn, the data is going to Agricola for the indexing and abstracting databases, since our catalogers have both the language and the subject expertise. If the NAL project spurs similar efforts in other libraries, demand for indexing and abstracting training for catalogers might become common.

All of this argues for a very broad interpretation of cataloging. It reinforces the notion that we are re-interpreting cataloging as bibliographic control and beyond bibliographic control to indexing and abstracting systems. We must reorganize cataloging operations to avoid compartmentalizing the people who work in them, because they need the broadest possible perspective. Equally important, we must redefine cataloging toward a content orientation, rather than a production orientation, to be able to use technology effectively.

There are several practical tips on how to work these ideas into staff training. The first thing I recommend is to find people within the library who are excited about the prospect of implementing change and use them as "seed" people to generate waves of positive reinforcement. Age and rank are less important than outlook. In my previous position, the head of cataloging was 63 years old and she was very excited about seeing online catalog and authority control systems in place before she retired. This was the capstone of her career. In the paraprofessional ranks, there are people who love working with computers. Turn them loose, for they will be truly creative and have a deeper understanding of the potential and the implications of different decisions.

Good training for the future will require time away from routine duties to experiment and integrate various systems and concepts. Training from the networks can be helpful. OCLC is experimenting with computer-aided training for their new software, while regional networks, such as CARL, are beginning to put their documentation out on floppy disks in a draft form that facilitates inserting individualized details to suit local needs.

Another approach is to encourage staff to go to users' groups and discussion groups, sponsored by professional associations and computer system vendors. American Library Association divisions such as the Library and Information Technology Association (LITA) and Association for Library Collections and Technical Services (ALCTS) do an excellent job of providing discussion groups. The smaller the group, the more helpful it is in sharing experiences at a very detailed level. To encourage participation, administrators must provide money for registration and travel fees.

I am arguing for a very broad role for catalogers. Catalogers' input into developing electronic systems should be seen as an essential part of the planning process, and provision must be made for their participation. In large libraries where some staff spend the majority of their time cataloging, direct access to planning for new systems will take effort to provide. Nevertheless, their participation gives a conceptual basis for catalog work as well as an opportunity to accept new ideas . Training for work with developing systems is no spectator sport; it requires active participation in an open environment.

MICHAEL FITZGERALD, Principal Cataloger, Harvard College Library.

I wish to begin by relieving the suspense created by an error in my printed paper and telling you how the last sentence on page 343 should end. The page lists two of the three characteristics of the Harvard University bibliographic standard--it names *AACR, LCSH,* or *MeSH* as descriptive and subject cataloging standards, respectively, and mandates acquisition record descriptions be based on International Standard Bibliographic Description--but breaks off before completing the third, concerning duplicate records.[1] The answer is that duplicate records are not allowed.

I am a member of the cataloging and processing department at Harvard College Library, the largest cataloging unit in the university's library. When I joined Widener (the library of Harvard College) almost a quarter of a century ago, we had a card catalog that was controlled by the catalog department and consisted primarily of catalog records. We followed local descriptive cataloging practice, had our own classification system, and our own subject heading system. Today, the catalog has, in a sense, been swallowed up by HOLLIS, the Harvard On-Line Library Information System. Records are created for HOLLIS by units throughout the library in collection development, in public services for the automated circulation, and by units small and large across the university. We also have records in HOLLIS that come from outside the university, e.g., Center for Research Library records, Boston Theological Consortium records, and records that are added whenever it is possible to tape load them. The database, as something under the control of the catalog department, has disappeared.

---

[1] Michael Fitzgerald, "Training the Cataloger: A Harvard Experience," in *Recruiting, Educating, and Training Cataloging Librarians: Solving the Problems,* ed. by Sheila S. Intner and Janet Swan Hill (Westport: Greenwood Press, 1989), p. 341-53.

Now, our cataloging unit subscribes to national standards. In 1978, we became participants in CONSER, the Conservation of Serials database building program; and in 1983, we entered into an agreement with the Library of Congress so that we are online directly with them and contribute catalog records directly into their bibliographic system, MUMS.[2]

The cataloger new out of library school is entering this world, and the most efficient way we have found to bring the cataloger to the point where he or she can contribute constructively and independently to the work of the department is through the use of a reviser, an experienced senior cataloger assigned on a one-to-one basis to review and correct their work, who will be able to provide the person with both the big picture and the small. An informal poll of the symposium audience showed that about half of those who received training to do cataloging were trained by revisers, demonstrating that this method goes far beyond the confines of Harvard.

In training the monograph cataloger, the reviser's first goal is to bring the cataloger to an awareness of all the documentation of the content of the bibliographic record, including *AACR2R*, Library of Congress rule interpretations, OCLC documentation, etc., and later, as the cataloger becomes more experienced, the Library of Congress's descriptive cataloging manual, the classification manuals, and subject heading manuals. The reviser tries to develop the habit of research, so that over time the trainee can come to appreciate what Noam Chomsky called "rule governed creativity". We appreciate working within this disciplined environment in order to achieve the major goal of bibliographic control.

The second thing we do is have the beginning monograph cataloger work at library assistant activities, and we do it for two

---

[2] The program through which Harvard contributes to the MUMS file is the National Coordinated Cataloging Project, described in detail by Henriette D. Avram and Beacher Wiggins in their article, "The National Coordinated Cataloging Program," *Library Resources & Technical Services* 32 (April 1988):111-15.

reasons: We want him or her to understand the mechanics of handling both OCLC and HOLLIS as well as to develop an appreciation for what our library assistants do. By being assigned to library assistant activities, new catalogers have more direct experience with the complex HOLLIS database than they might otherwise have. Furthermore, it is inevitable that a professional cataloger will supervise library assistants at some point, so this assignment helps them gain an awareness that the bulk of our production comes from the work of library assistants.

Finally, we are concerned about orientation. We want people to develop a sense of where they are, so we encourage them to attend orientation sessions at the university level. From the beginning, new people are encouraged go to anything the university library supplies, to the tour of Widener given by the reference department, and, as each HOLLIS innovation is introduced, to open meetings, discussions, and educational sessions on these enhancements. Thus, monograph catalogers become familiar with the general library community at Harvard.

Serial catalogers progress along a different track. Because we are CONSER participants, serial catalogers must work with all the CONSER documentation right from the beginning. They start out with Library of Congress records, but given the nature of serials, half of these records require some kind of change. When they are deemed ready, new serial catalogers move on to work with OCLC member records, which also involves learning Name Authority Cooperative (NACO) work, because Harvard is a self-authenticating CONSER participant. Finally, they move on to original cataloging. Ideally, serial catalogers are given daily revision because it is so important for them to receive timely feedback, but often it is very difficult for revisers to meet that goal.

Aside from the differences in the pattern of training, the monograph cataloger works more-or-less solely with automated systems. Serial cataloging is not as advanced, so it is important for serial catalogers to master both online and manual catalogs, including the serial card file, which also is an authority file, and the visible record of serial receipts. Serial catalogers have one foot in the old manual world and one foot in the new automated world.

At some point during the first year, usually when there are enough new catalogers already comfortable with descriptive cataloging, Peter Lisbon, chief subject cataloger, introduces them to the Library of Congress Classification (LCC). Peter gives two series of classes, the first teaching the schedules of the LCC and the old Widener classes still in use, supplemented by shelflist browsing to learn how numbers are constructed, and the second focusing on classification practice, including intensive work with the Library of Congress's *Subject Cataloging Manual*. Although the trainees are cataloging and classifying everything that they handle by this time, Peter continues revising them for about a year because he has found that misunderstandings may only surface after several months.

During the entire training process, trainees work with "real" materials. There is no collection of test books. Generally, revisers begin by assigning simple books, avoiding multipart works, corporate entries, etc., and then move on to Library of Congress cataloging copy, which affords an opportunity to concentrate on the interrelationship of bibliographic records, authority records, and other records in the file (i.e., acquisition records, circulation records, etc.). We place a high priority on file maintenance, because we are the most highly trained professionals handling the database.

Communication and evaluation of a person's performance is one of the most important areas in revision-based training. Too frequently in the past (and I have been guilty of this myself), we did not sit down to talk to people about their overall performance--about the good as well as the bad. Instead, we communicated with very brief, terse notes that pointed out errors. Some revisers find it difficult to have longer conversations about performance, but with practice it gets easier. One is very self-conscious at first, giving people regular evaluations and discussing their progress with them, but I think it is essential to make the revision process work most effectively. As a manager, I think it is essential, because it helps us make decisions about personnel.

This first year of cataloging service is one in which a foundation is being laid for the person's entire future career at Harvard and beyond. It takes time to grasp fully each element in the complex bibliographic control structure, and still more effort to understand their integration into an overall picture. Both are essential before new staff are prepared to make effective contributions to the work of the library.

MAUREEN SULLIVAN, Head, Library Personnel Services and Head, Processing Services, March 1989 to June 1990, Yale University.

Karin Trainer, Associate University Librarian, wisely ended her written paper for this Symposium (included in *Recruiting, Educating, and Training Cataloging Librarians*[3]) by saying that she expected that Gerald Lowell, Head of Technical Services, would be at a point in the implementation of Yale's planned reorganization where he would be able to join her in making her oral presentation, expanding on it and offering comments. He is not here, nor is Karin. I am here as the representative from Yale University to explain to you where we are now in that reorganization. As someone who has spent her library career as a personnel and training specialist, most of the remarks about the reorganization, beyond explaining its basic elements, are going to focus on training needs, particularly for catalogers.

Nancy Eaton emphasized the importance of interdisciplinary approaches to organizational change, particularly regarding technology. The fact that I am a personnel specialist, not a technical services librarian, taking the place of Karin Trainer who is our

---

[3] Karin A. Trainer, "Dollars and Sense: Training Catalogers," in *Recruiting, Educating, and Training Cataloging Librarians,* p. 367-74.

public services Associate University Librarian, and reporting to you on the work, the accomplishments, the ideas, and the vision of Gerald Lowell, head of technical services, is living proof that we at Yale are taking an interfunctional, if not an interdisciplinary, approach to the topic of preparing catalogers. I offer a practical implementation of some of the ideas that have been explored during the Symposium, particularly in this last session. I imagine, having just completed my second week as temporary Head of Processing Services, it might be difficult for you to believe that anything I have to say is practical. A good bit of our plans seem still to be at the theoretical level. However, we have taken advantage of an opportunity to put in place ideas I have heard presented by other speakers.

All of this is the result of a need and a decision to reorganize the technical services division in the Yale University Libraries, a division of almost 200 individuals, that was organized in the traditional way for many years. One of the significant changes in the reorganization is that we are moving away from a separate catalog and acquisition operation--and, by the way, the catalog department included serials--to a new structure with two major departments: Processing Services, made up of twelve teams; and the Database Management Department, the concept mentioned by several speakers.

The Database Management Department has two teams with about eighteen or nineteen staff total, while Processing Services with its twelve teams--the department I will head temporarily for the next year or so--has about 120 to 125 people. My best guess is that there are about forty librarians in the latter group. The particular significance of the reorganization for the cataloging librarians at Yale is that it is one of several changes they have experienced in the last several years. We are in the process of implementing NOTIS, although at Yale we call it ORBIS. The planning and decision-making process for the NOTIS implementation was a very participative one. We had almost ninety people participating formally in task forces or working groups. Of those ninety people, about two-thirds were from technical services. The others came from public service areas. It probably was the first time we had planned, formal interaction in such a broadly based decision-making process between public services and technical services librarians.

We recently introduced a new set of performance expectations for librarians at Yale that requires professional activities and professional growth and development, and assumes these things will be documented and recognized in a very careful, formal promotion structure.

There is another change in our environment, one that I call a cultural change. The best and strongest signal of the cultural change is the team approach we are taking to reorganization. The teams I describe are what Richard Hackman defined recently as self-managing work groups,[4] a concept I am told comes originally from experiences in European countries, particularly in Yugoslavia. Experiences in the United States with this concept to date have been concentrated in factory settings, primarily in the automobile industry. One of the significant differences in what we are doing at Yale, based upon what we have learned thus far, is that in preparing staff for this change, we are focusing as much on interpersonal, human relations skills training and group experience, development training as we are on the technical or job skills training that needs to take place for the reorganization.

Among the twelve teams that are going to comprise Processing Services, about half of the team leaders have not had previous supervisory or management experience. The other half were heads of units under the old structure. This presents an interesting situation in which some individuals have the grounding and supervisory skills Karin Trainer addresses in her paper, while others

---

[4] Richard Hackman,"The Psychology of Self-management in Organizations,"in *Psychology and Work: Productivity Change and Employment,* edited by M.S. Pollack and R.O. Perloff (Washington: American Psychological Association, 1986), p. 85-136.

do not.[5] After my initial experiences with them, I believe they are all experts in what Karin describes as the technical skills or the theoretical training that is important for catalogers. The two areas in which we are focusing now are the set of leadership skills required for the team leaders and members, and training in what Karin refers to as "strategic skills" or strategic training for catalogers, which she describes as the skills needed to do planning and conduct research.[6] I would expand Karin's definition of stategic skills to include creative problem solving, analytical skills, and the ability to forecast changes in the work to be performed and respond appropriately, i.e., to be able to adjust workflow and alter task design to accommodate expected changes.

The training that has taken place up to this point for implementing the reorganization includes engaging Organization Design and Development, a firm based in Bryn Mawr, Pennsylvania, to do two different workshops. The first was a three-day workshop for team leaders that discussed managerial philosophy, approaches to motivating staff, and leadership styles, and provided training in how to develop a group of people into a team. There was a whole section covering how to assess training needs and how to plan for changes in job design based on the results of the needs assessment. Two weeks after the three-day leadership workshops, we had training for all the team members and their leaders. We brought the teams together for the first time, and they worked as teams in a two-day session led by the same firm. The two-day sessions provided the team members with their first experience in working together, and

---

[5] Karin Trainer says, "'Supervisory skills' . . . encompass all of those human resources abilities necessary to keep a work group moving forward. [T]he person must be able to teach . . . technical skills to others in an effective way, to communicate, to motivate, to make good hiring and evaluation decisions, and to create the kind of climate in which good work takes place." Ibid., p. 369.

[6] Linda Ackerman, "The Transformational Manager: Facilitating the Flow State," in *The 1984 Annual: Developing Human Resources,* edited by J. William Pfeiffer and Leonard D. Goodstein (La Jolla, Calif.: University Associates, 1984), p. 242-56.

helped them learn how to deal with differences and conflicts, and how to plan and make decisions about their work. Of course, these two-day sessions were simulations, and the real life test has yet to come. The team members also gained experience in communicating with one another and a much better grasp of what is meant by a self-managing work group, especially what are the roles and responsibilities of team members and team leaders in this new structure.

The training we did was supported by a grant from the Council on Library Resources. I believe the Council took a significant step by supporting this kind of fundamental change in library organization and that Yale's experience may have wide impact, at least within the academic library arena.

The training described above took place in January 1989. At that time, we thought we would implement our reorganization during the first week in February. We postponed the date shortly after training was completed to the first week in April. We now believe [i.e., on the 11th of March, 1989] we must stick with this date and move forward on April 3, 1989, making it Day 1 of the reorganization. We knew that implementation was not likely to take place in one day and always assumed it would take some time to get used to the reorganization, but we believe now that implementation itself will occur over the course of several weeks. The progress of our administrative reorganization is linked with the progress of NOTIS implementation. Thus, we are becoming expert in flow-state management, which seems to be the norm in our organization these days.

The changes our librarians are experiencing are providing opportunities for them, but, as earlier speakers have indicated, they also are causing some frustrations. In my two weeks as Head of Processing Services I noticed problems that were formerly "under the rug" or at the edge of the rug for the last several years all seem to be coming out. The set of skills I am drawing on now are the same ones I used as a personnel librarian.

Our current consideration, to which we devote a great deal of time, is task definition. Hackman defines task definition as the key responsibility of leadership in the self managing environment.[7] We are in the process of determining the tasks to be performed at the start of the reorganization, and doing this as a separate activity from determining the tasks that will be performed once we have implemented various functions of NOTIS.

I am learning a lot in this process. The most surprising thing for me thus far is that I am not the only one who does not understand the different approaches we have to serials and monographs cataloging. I made a flippant suggestion that a glossary would be helpful for me. Within a short time, it was clear to me that a glossary will be helpful to everyone in this process. We have a large group of people who have been doing very specialized work in a narrowly defined context for a long period of time. They are experts, but only for narrow areas. As we move into the teams, each of these experts will do a much broader kind of cataloging than they have done before.

One of the first challenges for the teams will be to evaluate the skills and abilities present among the members as they begin their work as teams, to determine what skills development needs to take place, and, then, to plan the training to furnish development in those skills. We know already that we will spend a considerable amount of time during the next year offering training on a regular basis in communications skills, interpersonal relations, experience working in groups, creative problem analysis and problem solving. We also will have to offer seminars in serials cataloging, monographs cataloging, and more work with the MARC format. The advantage to the second group of training seminars will be that the logical people to do them are the librarians themselves.

---

[7] J. Richard Hackman, "The Psychology of Self-management in Organizations."

I started a "train the trainers" program for NOTIS implementation, and those concepts will be applied now to the work of the teams. The team leaders believe it is important for them to learn all the tasks that will be performed in their teams. My responsibility is to let them proceed with that view and see what happens. I am skeptical that they will succeed, because I believe it is very difficult for one team leader to learn all of those tasks. One of the ways interdependence will occur in the team, I think, will be identifying the person who has a particular expertise, and deciding how best to draw upon it.

In planning for the new performance expectations for librarians, we coined the term "the multifaceted specialist". In my opinion, the first group of truly multifaceted specialists in the Yale libraries will be the cataloging librarians. We are calling on them to look at new ways of organizing and accomplishing their work, to look very carefully at their roles and responsibilities, to be in a position to provide leadership to other individuals. Some of the other librarians are fully supportive of the reorganization, while others are skeptical, uncertain, and fearful they are not going to be successful in the process. All of this will take place as we implement and integrate the new online system, which, in the Yale application, will have features that have not been tried in other libraries. It is taking place at a time when we have ratchetted up the performance expectations for librarians, a time when cataloging librarians are expected to contribute to public service programs. Our catalogers serve on the OPAC (Online Public Access Catalog) Assistance Desk in the Reference Department. They also will be learning and developing new skills in the personnel field, designing work, defining tasks, and, as mentioned earlier, developing not just an ability to monitor work as it is being performed, but to anticipate changes and make the necessary adjustments to the systems and structures we have in place. And they must do all this under my leadership, someone who has personnel expertise and training expertise, but whose only experience with cataloging took place in library school, thirteen years ago.

The situation has proven to be one in which we are all learning. I had no idea how much I would learn by coming to this Symposium. I imagined I would just deliver my remarks, explaining what is going on at Yale. It is very exciting to discover that we are implementing some of the forward-looking ideas suggested by the speakers who preceded me today. I hope you will watch for the talks that Gerald Lowell will soon be offering to give, and I am encouraging the participants in our reorganization to write about it. I believe our experiences at Yale may provide a model that is likely to have broad application, especially among academic libraries.

D. KATHRYN WEINTRAUB, Principal Cataloger, University of California, Irvine.

Off-the-shelf software can be helpful to catalog department managers by providing useful tools for the initial and ongoing training and development of cataloging librarians. In the paper I prepared for this Symposium,[8] the uses of Lotus 1-2-3 and dBASE files in providing material for individual and group training discussions at the University of California, Irvine, are described at some length. What might not be obvious from a reading of that chapter, which concentrates on the methodology, are the positive effects of their use.

Spreadsheets are useful in monitoring the work of individuals in order to provide a general measure of the quality of their work, to identify problem areas when these occur, and to demonstrate the relative changes over time in the work of individuals and the department as a whole. With much attention given over to

---

[8] D. Kathryn Weintraub, "Using Management Tools for Cataloging Discussions," in *Recruiting, Educating, and Training Cataloging Librarians,* p. 375-89.

problems, how might the process be seen as a positive one? First, one begins with the assumption that evaluations of individuals' work necessarily includes respect for the privacy of the data and the idea that the trainee-trainer relationship depends on mutual trust between the parties. Second, one needs to remember that in our situation we are dealing for the most part with experienced, practicing catalogers who are interested in enhancing their expertise, developing their knowledge, and fine-tuning skills that are at a very high level already. Individual catalogers do not compete with one another; they compete with themselves.

The set of spreadsheets that I use for keeping records on the quality of people's work are important for three different reasons: First of all, they really tell the catalogers they are getting much better in their work, because, in fact, my records have shown over the years that the catalogers in the department consistently have improved. The spreadsheets furnish hard evidence that error rates are lower every year. Secondly, spreadsheets help me identify what kinds of mistakes are being made, which gives me, as the trainer, the information I need to recognize little knowledge gaps a cataloger might have. Once the mistake is identified, it usually is easy to address, and, often, the cataloger will supply the solution with little outside help, something he or she cannot do if he or she has no idea what mistakes are being made. Third, the spreadsheets are a good tool to show the management of the library that progress is being made.

Perhaps more important is the process I use in working with a cataloger and his or her spreadsheet. The spreadsheets are the basis for private person-to-person discussions. They furnish the evidence for making specific suggestions to individual catalogers to remedy knowledge gaps that have shown up in their work. Sometimes, once the cataloger sees the spreadsheet, he or she does not have to be told what needs doing, and it becomes clear immediately that some interpretation they made is incorrect. The spreadsheet is not shared with anyone else, it is not publicized, nor discussed with anyone else without the person's consent.

When something on the spreadsheet is going to be counted for a formal evaluation, the cataloger is aware of it in advance and has agreed to the process. What happens is that I ask each cataloger at some time during the year to give me all of their work for a period of time so I can revise each record. In doing the revisions, I make a sheet in which I list all of my comments, such as which rules they ought to read or reread. I give the cataloger my tally showing what will be counted. If they think I have not been fair, they have time to negotiate the issue immediately, which they are very likely to do if they think it is wrong, because they know they are being counted. The sheet is not only a control for me; it is a control for the cataloger as well. Data is entered until about 100 records accumulate in the file, and the difficulty of the records is tracked simultaneously, e.g., a sheet might show an error rate of 19% for editing records from before 1967 (pre-AACR). The cataloging code is one of the variables we think of as causing special difficulties in editing a record. I examine the sheet with an eye toward distinguishing between errors that might be expected, e.g., in a type of record the cataloger has just started to do, and errors that should not be occurring, because the cataloger has had training and experience in doing that particular type of task. When the latter type of error surfaces, I spend time talking to the cataloger about correcting it, although it will not necessarily be the category in which he or she had the highest error rate.

Several speakers throughout the Symposium have said that catalogers are nit picking, always looking at details, etc., so I hasten to explain that the quality of cataloging done by an individual cataloger as represented in the spreadsheets is only one measure used and only one aspect of the evaluation process a librarian undergoes at Irvine. Catalogers are expected to do quality work, and the quantity of the work they do is also reviewed. They also are expected to contribute to the work of the department by making suggestions and being helpful. One of our library assistants developed a worksheet that is much more useful from the point of view of the catalogers than the one we formerly used. Two other library assistants, after they saw this draft, took one of our inputters out to lunch, and persuaded her that she would like this new worksheet. These kinds of things are included in the evaluation of a cataloger's work as very positive and significant contributions. It is never simply a matter of saying so-and-so had an error rate of 14.9%.

It is difficult to find objective measures of quality, and even these useful spreadsheets are not without problems. One problem is that everything one might like to count will not fit on the spreadsheet, particularly if you are unwilling to go to multiple pages for one person. One has to select which elements will not be included. Second, all the program does in providing error rates is calculate a ratio of mistakes to records prepared. If you have done any cataloging, you know that you do a great many things on a record correctly even when it contains a mistake. One mistake does not make a record 100% wrong, but that is what the spreadsheet shows. There are other distortions, too, explained in more detail in "Using Management Tools for Cataloging Discussions."[9] Nonetheless, the spreadsheets are a great deal better than alternatives that depend on a supervisor's opinions or personal impressions.

In conclusion, preparing data files containing objective data that can be useful to people is rewarding and is appreciated by the people to whom it applies. The Lotus files are much better than sheaves of worksheets, each containing one record, from which an impressionistic interpretation is derived. At the University of California, Irvine, catalogers try to do the best work they can, and the Lotus files are a tool that helps them. So long as the caveats

---

[9] Ibid., p. 382-84.

inherent in creating and using statistics are borne in mind, off-the-shelf software can be used to make a positive contribution in training catalogers.

The discussion following the third session was moderated by Karen Muller. She began by summarizing the main themes of each presentation, saying: "The thing we have learned this afternoon is that training takes time and appropriate tools. Henriette Avram pointed out that there is no quick fix. Michael Fitzgerald described the very long training process at Harvard with classes and other checks on development. Kathryn Weintraub provided us with some specific evaluation tools. Barbra Higginbotham suggested there needs to be a commitment to good training from the bibliographic utilities. Maureen Sullivan has described long term skills development that are important to make sure things happen as planned, and pointed out that delays occur in the best laid plans. Nancy Eaton said it takes time to understand the magnitude of the changes occurring in information technology and bibliographic control. Kathy Bales explained that training is a change agent." And, then, she opened the third and final discussion of the Symposium.

DISCUSSION #3
TRAINING CATALOGING
LIBRARIANS

Theme 1: Determining and accounting for an appropriate level of commitment in time and resources to plan for and conduct ongoing training, especially in large libraries.

Three points need to be considered concerning training in a very large institution, e.g., one the size of the Library of Congress (LC): (1) the training structure, which, at LC, is a highly formalized one, namely, the training of trainers who are responsible for training staff down the line; (2) the commitment of time of the trainers; and, (3) the level of commitment of the staff being trained.

At LC, where there are so many people to be trained, the approach has been taken of having a key trainer in each unit of processing services. By doing that--and even that takes time and effort away from other things and represents a large commitment--we spread training throughout the organization. The positions for the training organization have been filled, and equipment and supporting staff and materials are provided, but there are not enough people in LC's Technical Processing and Automation Instruction Office (TPAIO) to do everything that is needed in an institution of the size of LC.

The chief of LC's training office, Judy Cannan, is a former serials cataloger, not a professional trainer. She herself went through a lot of training classes, and out of this exposure came a need to know. She went into the job of chief of TPAIO enthusiastically, and she has done wonders.

At LC, the training commitment started principally with the key trainers themselves and the people concerned with automation in the different units of the department. In many instances, supervisors resented the training staff, but over a period of three years, that has changed and now they are most welcome. There was a little giving on both sides. Now there is a higher degree of commitment to training on the part of departmental staff in general. They call up to make requests for training that are overwhelming the abilities of the five people on the TPAIO staff to accommodate. Of course, there must be a reason if you are training. At LC we always establish the need prior to anything we do.

In general, the commitment to expend money, time, and staff for training has to be related to the value of that training--what one gets out of it. If the value of the training cannot be demonstrated by increases in the quality of bibliographic products and services, then the training itself cannot be justified. The benefits of training and the use to the library supporting it need to be clarified and made explicit.

Theme 2: Clarifying attitudes about cataloging errors: when is an error an error? what about cataloging errors?

There seems to be a difference in attitudes toward cataloging errors among the speakers. One speaker expressed contempt for catalogers who keep records of colleagues who do error-prone work, claiming there are reasonable variations in the interpretation of cataloging standards. Others have spoken at some length about how errors are carefully tracked and attempts made to eliminate them. What are we to do about training if one institution's objective is to achieve "error-free" cataloging, while another institution disputes that objective and accepts variations in interpretation of cataloging rules as properly within the individual cataloger's authority? Aside from typographical errors and misspellings, which everyone agrees are erroneous and tries to eliminate, when is a variation in applying cataloging standards an error, and not to be accepted?

If an error gets in the way of an item being found, it is important; otherwise, it is not. Some libraries send in error reports to their bibliographic utilities to take a period out or put a period in somewhere. Perhaps that represents the lowest end on a continuum of error importance.

Catalogs are used in two ways, however: First, they are used in the traditional way, where a patron comes up to a catalog and looks for a record and finds or doesn't find it. In this scenario, the only significant errors might be those occurring in access points. Another way catalogs are used, however, is by staff searchers trying to match an item in hand with a catalog record or to select material because it has certain characteristics. If elements other than retrieval points contain errors, say, because a cataloger miscounted the number of pages, an acquisitions librarian looking for a 420 page book might conclude quite reasonably that the record for a 398 page book was the wrong item. Thus, errors in parts of the record other than access points can be important, although not necessarily to all of the catalog's lay users. Researchers in some disciplines are interested in the materials represented by catalog records as physical artifacts. For these people, accuracy in elements other than the access points also assumes greater importance.

Two uses of records in online databases that require accuracy throughout the record, not solely in access points, are to teach and learn cataloging by emulating database records as authoritative, and to establish a local online catalog through use of a library's network archive tapes. In the former instance, beginning catalogers believe they can have confidence in the accuracy of online records because they are created, supposedly, by experienced professionals. No matter how many times a cataloging teacher warns students to believe what they hold in their hands, they still tend to prefer what they see on the screen. In the latter instance, if fixed fields have not been coded correctly or if errors occur in various fields, an enormously expensive editing job must be undertaken just to achieve a usable local catalog. One business rule of thumb catalogers might think about is that it is always more expensive to go back and redo something than to do it right in the first place. Librarians could benefit from consideration of long term goals when they establish cataloging policies.

Catalogers need to be liberated from an overriding concern about errors so they can look at the broader picture and provide records that do what we need them to do, which is to get people to the items. How can training help accomplish this?

Before Columbia University Libraries implemented the Research Libraries Information Network (RLIN), they had not had any previous form of automation. Catalogers had typed their records on 3x5 slips of paper interleaved with carbon. All at once, they began to see cataloging copy furnished by other network members. Catalogers in the original cataloging department were processing this member copy and correcting it to the nines as well as creating their own original records. After the staff grew accustomed to RLIN, it was suggested that it would be useful to establish a work group in the cataloging department, and have that group set up a chart, take every member copy record over a period of two or three months, and analyze which areas of the record required corrections. Then, the group was to weight the corrections according to a scale of their value to Columbia, and recommend whether the errors were significant enough to continue their workflow through original cataloging. It was important to determine whether or not Columbia could afford that level of scrutiny or whether they might have faith in the work of their colleagues in other libraries and let these records go to a copy cataloging unit. Once the analysis was performed, the decision was easily made to recommend to management that these records go to copy cataloging, and that staffing be adjusted. It was a great experience for the cataloging staff to be concerned about identifying problems and deciding how serious they were and how to proceed.

Similar experiences have happened elsewhere, e.g., at one library, the process called "final revision," the review before records went to the OCLC terminals for input, was investigated. In reviewing the errors being corrected by two high level cataloging librarians, it was learned that only occasionally did they find substantive errors of wrong entry, missing added entries, etc.; most of their work corrected obvious typographical or spelling errors that could have been caught by any good copy editor. As a result, this library is eliminating the high level catalogers' review. Perhaps when catalogers talk about errors, it is because they cannot quite get a handle on the underlying problems, but they hope focusing on error correction will result in raising the general concentration levels of the staff involved, sort of "shake them up" a bit and get them to work more attentively.

At RLIN, error reports are received, sorted, and sent back to the owning libraries. RLIN quality control staff only correct errors in LC's Cataloging-in-Publication records, because they want the reference to be clean. What RLIN members say is that they will correct errors in access points and, if there is time, they will correct the next level of error. Individual cataloging departments have criteria for what is important and what is not. If they can, they will get to the bottom of their lists; but, if they cannot, they cannot. RLIN staff feel they can only exert pressure on users to correct access points.

Catalogers and cataloging managers are extremely fortunate that there are such things as error counts, because counting one' errors, identifying them, and identifying patterns of error are valuable parts of the training process, and, occasionally, also in the evaluation process. Library managers are at a disadvantage that there is no similar mechanism available for reference librarians. There is no equivalent to the mis-tagging that results in a record's not being indexed properly and, therefore, lost that one can see in the case of a reference librarian giving poor, misleading, or incomplete answers to patron questions.

Theme 3: The impact of new organizational methods for performing needed tasks in cataloging and database maintenance.

A 1987 OCLC study of database quality surveyed librarians on what they perceived as the most important error correction taking place. They identified errors in access points first, followed by duplicate detection, and all other errors. As a result, OCLC reorganized its quality control section based on that priority scale. The reorganized staff worked in teams of professionals and paraprofessionals, and focused on subject headings, name headings, and duplicate records. In the last six months, they increased 51% in their productivity. If this activity continues for a year, extrapolating from the six month figures, we are going to correct more than 300,000 records online, one-by-one, which is a significant increase. Only two things that changed that might explain the enormous jump in productivity: the formation of quality circles; and the fact that the staff were working toward a goal that they believe meets their users' requirements.

If we are looking for new people to do cataloging, we have to look ahead to where we are going in the next ten years. Even though we agreed that we need to make cataloging exciting to attract people, here we are, talking about error counting instead of talking about the encouraging things. The Yale experiment shows learning, development, interest, growth, and change. These are the things we must do everywhere in order to attract people to cataloging. Cataloging has to have creativity, decisions to make, research, communication, and work with people as well as the traditional things, and we have to educate and train catalogers appropriately.

As technical service librarians, we have an obligation to think of new and innovative ways to use technology to solve our problems. One of the merits of the Yale experiment is that they have not approached their problems by changing the cataloging rules or coming up with some mythical way to organize data perfectly, but they are thinking of new ways to organize their operations, just as LC is seeking ways to reorganize for greater effectiveness.

Among the ways of employing technology in cataloging, a cataloger's workstation has been mentioned several times. The idea of digitizing the cataloging rules is under investigation by ALA and the British and Canadian library associations. Unfortunately, nothing much has happened since January, when the three publishers met with OCLC and LC to talk about a MARC format for cataloging rules. If such a format was devised, it could be integrated with similar formats for subject headings, rule interpretations, and classifications. Eventually, it will all happen, although it takes time.

Theme 4: Taking a broad approach to the catalog and systems development.

I hate to spend much time talking about error counting, because catalogers hate it, feeling it to be terribly demeaning, and for good reason. But this is one of the areas where the breadth of someone's understanding of the entire system is important, and why a broad approach to the catalog and systems development is essential. We may say that the only errors that count are in access points, but one discovers that what we actually mean is machine access, which is not the same as what we would have defined as access points only a year or two earlier. Machine access depends on what your particular automation system can acquire, can seek, can sort by. People used to think that the fixed fields (i.e., MARC format field 008) were a total waste of time, but automated systems can retrieve groups of materials via the fixed fields. If your library made the mistake of not counting errors in the fixed fields, you will retrieve fascinating combinations this way. If you believed that accurate fixed field coding was not worth spending your training time on, you'll never be able to retrieve those materials.

Theme 5: The training role of professional associations, library school continuing education programs, etc.

None of the speakers at this Symposium have addressed the role of professional associations or library school-sponsored continuing education and training beyond the master's degree. Libraries that have only one cataloger must look to training activities outside their library. Are these outside training opportunities useful? Do people find them helpful? What sources do they seek? Do they send their catalogers out to workshops, institutes, or courses, or do they bring in consultants, or rely on the expertise of in-house staff?

On the basis of the experiences of the American Library Association's (ALA) Resources and Technical Services Division (now called the Association for Library Collections and Technical Services), there is a large response to continuing education institutes whenever they cover very practical training, e.g., how to use *AACR*, how to use *LCSH*, how to classify, etc. We get sellout crowds, which suggests this kind of training is highly desired.

OCLC, at least the Pacific Coast Network (PACNET), has a very active program of workshops taught by experienced professionals. PACNET even videotapes the workshops and makes them available. Anything that is practical, including discussion groups at ALA conferences, draws people in droves.

As a librarian in a one-person special library, I have found outside workshops essential to keep up with rule changes, uniform access to software, etc. Most of the presentations in the Symposium's training session were geared to large cataloging departments in academic libraries. I just want to emphasize that in small libraries, the same standards and the same needs in training and education are important so that these libraries can stay in the mainstream and contribute to the conglomeration of networks we call the national network.

Theme 6: Issues of the one-person library.

The problem of the one-person operation, or the one-person cataloging operation is what makes the quality of the education and training available in the graduate library school so worrisome. People who leave a graduate library school program with a master's degree are hired by people to run their libraries, and those librarians have to rely on what they acquired in library school to get them through. Many do just fine, albeit painfully, and they may feel extremely unsure of themselves for a long time. This should be a considerable concern not only for managers of large libraries, but also for the library schools. The library school is the only place the librarian-cataloger in a one-person operation is going to get any training, even though it is generally agreed that master's degree programs should emphasize education.

Most library schools try to inculcate into their graduates that the master's degree is only the beginning of their careers, not the end. They have to make sure that every student who leaves the library school understands that what they have is only the beginning of their professional life. In order to continue in the profession, they must continue learning, whether they do it on their own, through professional associations, or any other type of continuing education. If someone takes a position where they spend one-quarter of their time cataloging and they feel insecure about doing it, they should get the information they need in order to do the kind of job they should be doing.

The idea for training internships described in "Standards, Volume, and Trust in the Shared Cataloging Environment"[1] did not come out of a vacuum. It came from my [i.e., Dr. Barbra Higginbotham's] experience as an administrator of an original cataloging department where many art materials were cataloged. We were fortunate to obtain grant money for cataloging projects, and in pulling materials out of the backlog, we began to see more and more member copy from small museum librarians using RLIN. The catalogers using the records complained that the museum-contributed records were worse than nothing and took longer to edit than starting from scratch. Then an idea surfaced: Perhaps we should call these places up and tell them if they were willing to send someone over to us, we would teach them how to catalog. Then they could return to their libraries and do it right. The lack of knowledge of the small special librarian is not just a problem for the individual library, but for all the members of the same network who are entitled to receive good quality cataloging.

No one ever talks about it, but there is a proportion of records in network databases that are done by people who are not librarians and who have never had a library school course in cataloging. It is very difficult to determine how many records such as these there are in

---

[1] Barbra Buckner Higginbotham, "Standards, Volume, and Trust in the Shared Cataloging Environment: Training Approaches for the Smaller Library," in *Recruiting, Educating, and Training Cataloging Librarians,* 355-66.

the networks, because, if asked, who would want to admit their cataloging was done by someone with no cataloging knowledge? Continuing education that is easily accessible in libraries, perhaps distance education, is essential to address this need.

Theme 7: Licensing and certification of cataloging librarians.

Other professions have licensing examinations and certification to insure that their practitioners are competent and meet certain standards. Is there a place for this in cataloging? If joining a bibliographic utility meant you had to hire certified catalogers, small libraries could not hire untrained catalogers and by doing so cost their larger library colleagues the extra money it takes to edit poor cataloging. We assume that the larger libraries are putting the money into appropriate training, but certification could insure that they do not neglect it, either. Now we have no way of controlling the quality of training that is given. After all, accreditation is supposed to control the quality of education, but there is nothing comparable for on-the-job training.

Theme 8: Balancing local and national needs.

There are tradeoffs between local and national needs, and each institution has the right to choose for itself where to draw the line between them. Managers should analyze the costs and benefits of various levels of training to arrive at a viable measure of commitment for their local institution, provided the decision does not negate standard expectations. At the same time, since we can only approach perfection in our databases rather than achieve it, we ought to recognize the level of error we are willing to accept and live with, and the level to which we must be opposed, because it hampers our activities.

Theme 9: Educators and practitioners need to work together to solve problems in recruiting, educating, and training cataloging librarians.

One of the most valuable things about a symposium such as this one is that it brings together people who are full time in education and people who are full time in practice. This is one of several good methods practitioners have to tell library school faculty what they think students should be learning. While faculty may not do exactly what practitioners say, they listen. Faculty are very receptive to expressions of interest by practitioners, and changes can be effected, e.g., in distance learning. Certification is not such a bad idea, either. If somebody wants to develop an examination for the certification of catalogers, there would be faculty members interested in looking at it, too. These are activities of major importance.

Going back to the beginning of the conference, our prime need is for people who will help us look ahead and develop recruitment. By relying on recruiting those people who have already tripped over our threshold, we restrict ourselves to a continuation of the status quo, in which not enough people come in who are interested in cataloging--even cataloging defined as making the plans and creative thought to lead us to the future. The library can be a laboratory and a recruitment mechanism itself. If we do things that are exciting, people will hear interesting things are going on in our library, and we will reach them.

If practitioners identify their objectives and do more empirical research on how to reach them, it will help educators do a better job of focusing on the things of greatest importance in the long run, not just making incremental improvements at the moment. There is a crying need for empirical research in library science and not many people do it. Catalogers are particularly hard-pressed to do needed research because of the work environment in which they find themselves. They sit in a open room full of paraprofessionals who are paid by the hour, and they are responsible for making sure the supervisees do not read magazines at their desks while the catalogers try to do professional reading at theirs. Productivity is measured in numbers, and quotas have to be met. Who can they find the time or the place to do research? There certainly are not enough cataloging professors to do all the needed research, and not enough catalogers to do all the work. It seems to be an impossible situation, one that library administrators must address.

Practitioners can infiltrate educators' groups, such as the Association for Library and Information Science Education (ALISE) and talk about what they need, and find out what problems the educators are having. Three years ago, I got up in front of a group of 100 catalogers and said, "I am having trouble recruiting people. Are you?" And they all said, "Yes, but I thought it was just me." Then we started to survey the situation, to write about it, to form an ALA task force that is now a standing committee, and talk to educators. Eventually, some of us joined ALISE. Now I go to ALISE meetings and I infiltrate. A Special Interest Group on Technical Service Education was begun and the last meeting found a growing group of practitioners in the audience in addition to many educators. Other practitioners should consider doing the same.

Not all library school faculties are receptive to talking to practitioners or having practitioners talk to their students. One library school dean I contacted said someone would get in touch with me, but they never did. Finally, being an administrator with positions to fill, I contacted the placement service of the university and talked to the library science students on Career Day. The students had a host of misconceptions about libraries. They believed all sorts of myths about how to fill out a résumé and who hires whom for what reasons. I suggested they get some experience, particularly in technical services. They had never heard this before; they heard the opposite. They heard people say, "Don't go into cataloging or acquisitions. Those are not professional jobs." Library schools do not routinely bring in people to tell students what the job market is like, and the importance of getting practical experience. There also is a great deal of bad advice about career paths being given by professors.

One objective of the Council on Library Resources-funded Senior Fellows Project is to provide interaction between library educators and practitioners. In my group, we felt that was not happening in a substantial way. One thing I have done since then was to volunteer to be an accreditation team site visitor, because perhaps practitioners have been remiss in not being more involved in dialog on curriculum development. That is a small personal step, but those kinds of things add up. One benefit is that you and the educators discover you are not the enemy--either one of you--and eventually you discover you both are interested in the same things.

Library educators and practitioners need to talk to each other. Practitioners and administrators should not only express their needs, which are absolutely essential for faculty to hear, but also take the time to listen to the faculty dream their dreams. Listen to faculty deal with tough issues in research that have nothing to do with practice, but which represent the dreams of our field for the next ten or fifteen years. There has got to be a reciprocity. I am convinced that the research in our field is moving away from library schools and going into places such as OCLC. Practitioners have much to gain from dreaming these more remote and esoteric dreams, not just the dreams about what they need to run their particular library.

The conclusion.

What we learned in earlier sessions is that we have to make cataloging activities attractive. We need to market what we do so we can recruit not our clones, but people who have the skills we will need in the future. We learned about educating these people in a relevant way and giving them a solid foundation plus the motivation to continue learning for the future. And, in this session, we found that after they are graduated from our schools, we must define their training needs in ways that insure they have the skills to work in the libraries of the future, because the libraries of the future will not be the institutions we know today.

SELECTED BIBLIOGRAPHY

Compiled by Sheila S. Intner

This bibliography updates the one that appeared in *Recruiting, Educating, and Training Cataloging Librarians* and does not duplicate items listed there. With a few exceptions, the list below is limited to English-language works published in 1988 or later.

GENERAL WORKS

American Library Association. Office for Library Personnel Resources. *Each One Reach One: Recruiting for the Profession Action Handbook.* Chicago: American Library Association, 1989.

Auld, Lawrence W. S. "Seven Imperatives for Library Education." *Library Journal* 115 (May 1, 1990):55-59.

Brenda White Associates. *Education and Recruitment of Junior Professionals: A Study in the Library and Information Profession.* Great Britain: British Library, 1989.

Buttlar, Lois and Rosemary R. DuMont. "Assessing Library Science Competencies: Soliciting Practitioner Input for Curriculum Design." *Journal of Education for Library and Information Science Education* 30 (Summer 1989):3-18.

Cluff, E. Dale, editor. "Library Education and Employer Expectations." *Journal of Library Administration* 11, nos. 3/4 (1990). [Also published as a separate, monographic book with the title *Library Education and Employer Expectations.*]

Creth, Sheila. *Effective On-the-job Training: Developing Library Human Resources.* Chicago: American Library Association, 1986.

Davenport, Lizzie and Blaise Cronin. "Demand and Supply in Information Work." *Education for Information* 6 (March 1988):61-70.

Gherman, Paul M. and Frances O. Painter, editors. "Training Issues and Strategies in Libraries." *Journal of Library Administration* 12, no. 2 (1990). [Also published as a separate, monographic book with the title *Training Issues and Strategies in Libraries.*]

Glogoff, Stuart, editor. "Staff Training in the Automated Library Environment: A Symposium." *Library Hi Tech* 7, no. 4 (1989):61-83.

Healey, James S. "The Electronic Library School: An Alternative Approach in Library Education." *Technical Services Quarterly* 6, no. 2 (1988):17-26.

Heyser, Teresa and Richard G. Heyser. "The Role of Library
    Education in Meeting the Personnel Needs of Public and
    School Libraries." *Journal of Library Administration* 10,
    no. 4 (1989):3-19. [The entire issue, edited by Gisela Webb,
    is devoted to "Human Resources Management in Libraries."
    The Heysers' article is particularly useful.]

Kirkland, Janice. "Recruitment and Education." *Library Personnel
    News* 3 (Summer 1989):41-42.

Krantz, Charles E., et al. *Training Issues in Changing Technology.*
    Chicago: American Library Association, Library
    Administration and Management Association, 1986.

Leinbach, Philip E., editor. "Personnel Administration in an
    Automated Environment." *Journal of Library
    Administration* 13, nos. 1/2 (1990). [In press; will also be
    available as a monograph.]

Library of Congress. Technical Processing and Automation
    Instruction Office. "Training the Trainer: Manual"
    (Unpublished typescript) [Manual originally prepared for
    use at the Library for technical training, including cataloging
    and classification and automation, currently in press.]

Library Personnel News. Chicago: American Library Association,
    Office for Library Personnel Resources, 1987- [Quarterly
    newsletter]

Lipow, Anne G. "Training for Change: Staff Development in a
    New Age." *Journal of Library Administration* 10, no. 4
    (1989).

Moen, William E. and Kathleen M. Heim. *Librarians for the New Millenium*. Chicago: American Library Association, Office for Library Personnel Resources, 1988.

Poa, Miranda Lee and Robert M. Warner. "Strategic Planning for the 1990s: A Challenge for Change." *Education for Information* 7 (Sept. 1989):263-71.

Rubin, Richard, editor. "Personnel Management in Libraries." *Library Trends* 38 (Summer 1989):1-151. [Essays of special interest include "Managing Resistance to Change," by Sharon L. Baker; "Organizational Entry: Human Resources Selection and Adaptation in Response to a Complex Labor Pool," by Kathleen M. Heim; and "Why Training Doesn't Stick: Who Is to Blame?" by Anne G. Lipow.]

White, Herbert S. *Librarians and the Awakening from Innocence: A Collection of Papers*. Boston: G. K. Hall, 1989.

WORKS FOCUSING ON CATALOGING AND TECHNICAL SERVICES

Bishoff, Liz. "Job Analysis" in "Shall We Throw Out the Technical Services--And Then What?" edited by D. Kathryn Weintraub. *Library Resources & Technical Services* 34 (July 1990), in press.

Carter, Ruth C., editor. "Education and Training for Catalogers and Classifiers." *Cataloging & Classification Quarterly* 7, no. 4 (Summer 1987):1-163. [Entire issue is of interest; a few of the articles were listed in the bibliography in *Recruiting, Educating, and Training Cataloging Librarians*. Also available as a monograph, titled *Education and Training for Catalogers and Classifiers*.]

"Cataloging Librarians Address Staffing Needs." *Library
    Personnel News* 3 (Summer 1989):40. [Report of the
    Simmons College Symposium on Recruiting, Educating, and
    Training Cataloging Librarians.]

Hill, Janet Swan. "Stalking the Elusive Cataloger." *American
    Libraries* 20 (May 1989):458+. [Report of the Simmons
    College Symposium on Recruiting, Educating, and Training
    Cataloging Librarians.]

Intner, Sheila S. "Preaching the Word: Recruiting Catalogers at
    Simmons Symposium." *Library Journal* 114 (April 15,
    1989):12. [Report of the Simmons College Symposium on
    Recruiting, Educating, and Training Cataloging Librarians.]

---------- and Cecilia Piccolo. "Practical and Theoretical Knowledge
    in Cataloging: What We Should Teach and Why" in *Théorie
    et Practique dans l'Enseignement des Sciences de
    l'Information,* edited by Réjean Savard. Montreal:
    AIESI/ALISE Joint Colloquium, 1988, p. 259-84.

Kershner, Lois. "Training People for New Job Responsibilities: The
    Lesson Plan" in "Shall We Throw Out the Technical
    Services--And Then What?" edited by D. Kathryn Weintraub.
    Library Resources & Technical Services 34 (April
    1990):251-55.

Kovacs, Beatrice. "An Educational Challenge: Teaching Cataloging
    and Classification." *Library Resources & Technical
    Services* 33 (Oct. 1989):374-81.

McCombs, Gillian M. "Public and Technical Services: The Hidden
    Dialectic." *RQ* 28 (Winter 1988):141-45.

Peters, Stephen H. "Time Devoted to Topics in Cataloging Courses." *Journal of Education for Library and Information Science Education* 29 (Winter 1989):209-19.

Rapp, Joan. "Personnel Selection for Cataloging" in "Shall We Throw Out the Technical Services--And Then What?" edited by D. Kathryn Weintraub. *Library Resources & Technical Services* 34 (Jan. 1990):95-99.

Spivey, Barbara. *Training in Cataloging: A Review of the First Year.* ERIC, 1987. ED 307 873.

Webb, Gisela M. "Strategies for Recruiting Technical Services Personnel." *Technicalities* 8 (Nov. 1988):13-15.

Weinberg, Bella Hass. "A Graduate-level Course on Hebraica Cataloging." *Judaica Librarianship* 4 (1987-88):85-88.

INDEX

ABOUT THE EDITORS

SHEILA S. INTNER is a Professor in the Graduate School of Library and Information Science at Simmons College, Boston, Massachusetts, where she teaches courses in cataloging and classification, collection development, and bibliographic instruction. Dr. Intner's recent books include *Standard Cataloging for School and Public Libraries* (Libraries Unlimited, 1990), *Library Education and Leadership* (Scarecrow, 1990), *Recruiting, Educating, and Training Cataloging Librarians* (Greenwood, 1989), *The Library Microcomputer Environment* (Oryx, 1988), and *Circulation Policy in Academic, School, and Public Libraries* (Greenwood, 1987). Dr. Intner edited *Library Resources & Technical Services* from 1987 to 1990. She writes the bimonthly "Interfaces" column for *Technicalities* and edits a monographic series for ALA Books titled *Frontiers of Access to Library Materials*. Chair of ALA's 1991 Margaret Mann Citation Award Committee, Dr. Intner previously chaired the Cataloging and Classification Section of the Resources and Technical Services Division. Dr. Intner received an MLS in 1976 from Queens College, Flushing, New York, and a DLS in 1982 from Columbia University in New York City.

JANET SWAN HILL is Associate Director for Technical Services at the University of Colorado's Norlin Library in Boulder where she directs library bibliographic control systems and services. Ms. Hill was recently appointed the American Library Association's voting reprsentative to the international Joint Steering Committee for Revision of AACR, where she casts one of the two votes accorded to the United States of America. (The other is cast by Ben R. Tucker for the Library of Congress.) Ms. Hill was a founding member of the Special Interest Group on Technical Services Education of the Association for Library and Information Science Education as well as the American Library Association's Committee on Education, Training, and Recruitment for Cataloging, established as a result of her research into the shortage of catalogers. Her recent publications include *Recruiting, Educating, and Training Cataloging Librarians* (Greenwood, 1989) and numerous articles on cataloging, catalog management, networking, and related topics. Ms. Hill received her MLS in 1971 from the University of Denver.

ABOUT THE CONTRIBUTORS

HENRIETTE D. AVRAM is Associate Librarian for Collections Services at the Library of Congress, Washington, DC.

LIZ BISHOFF is Manager of Cataloging and Database Services at OCLC, Inc., Dublin, Ohio.

MICHAEL CARPENTER is an Assistant Professor at the School of Library and Information Science, Louisiana State University, Baton Rouge.

D. WHITNEY COE is Anglo-American Bibliographer at Firestone Library, Princeton University, Princeton, New Jersey.

NANCY L. EATON is Director of Library Services at Iowa State University, Ames.

MICHAEL FITZGERALD is the Principal Cataloger at Widener Library, Harvard College, Cambridge, Massachusetts.

CAROLYN O. FROST is a Professor and Associate Dean of the School of Information and Library Studies, University of Michigan, Ann Arbor.

ELIZABETH FUTAS is Director of the Graduate School of Library and Information Studies at the University of Rhode Island, Kingston.

ROBERT M. HAYES, Dean and Professor of the Graduate School of Library and Information Science at UCLA until his retirement in 1989, is a consultant and advisor to OCLC, Inc., on matters pertaining to research libraries.

SUZANNE HILDENBRAND is an Associate Professor in the School of Information and Library Studies at the State University of New York, Buffalo.

HEIDI LEE HOERMAN, formerly Assistant Dean for Technical Services at Montana State University Libraries, is now a doctoral student at the School of Library and Information Science, Indiana University, Bloomington.

BEATRICE KOVACS is an Assistant Professor in the Department of Library and Information Studies at the University of North Carolina, Greensboro.

THOMAS W. LEONHARDT is Dean of Library Services at the University of the Pacific, Stockton, California.

JAMES M. MATARAZZO is a Professor in the Graduate School of Library and Information Science at Simmons College, Boston, Massachusetts.

JOSEPH R. MATTHEWS is Vice President and General Manager of GEAC International, Markham, Ontario.

FRANCIS MIKSA is a Professor in the Graduate School of Library and Information Science at the University of Texas, Austin.

JAMES G. NEAL is Director of University Libraries at Indiana University, Bloomington.

MARION T. REID is Director of Library Services at the California State University, San Marcos.

JANE B. ROBBINS is a Professor and Director of the School of Library and Information Studies at the University of Wisconsin, Madison.

MAUREEN SULLIVAN is Head of Personnel Services and Temporary Head of Processing Services at Yale University Libraries, New Haven, Connecticut.

D. KATHRYN WEINTRAUB is Principal Cataloger at the University Library, University of California, Irvine.

FAY ZIPKOWITZ is an Associate Professor in the Graduate School of Library and Information Studies at the University of Rhode Island, Kingston.

MEMBERS OF THE SYMPOSIUM AUDIENCE

Anne M. Acton, New England School of Law Library, Boston, MA
Allan Allaire, Simmons College, Boston, MA
Sarah Alleman, Lane Public Library, Hamilton, OH
Joanna Andrews, McGill University, Montreal, QB
Mildred M. Bader, University of Washington, Seattle, WA
Judith B. Barnett, University of Rhode Island, Narragansett, RI
Emily L. Beattie, Waltham, MA
Christina Bellinger, Massachusetts State Library, Boston, MA
Martha Beshers, University of Connecticut, Storrs, CT
Elizabeth Bishai, Harvard University, Cambridge, MA
Victoria M. Blair-Smith, Buckingham Browne & Nichols School,
    Cambridge, MA
Jacqueline Byrd, Indiana University, Bloomington, IN
Karen Carlson, Harvard College Library, Cambridge, MA
Co-ming Chan, Oklahoma State University Library, Stillwater, OK
Lois Mai Chan, University of Kentucky, Lexington, KY
Belinda Chiang, Harvard Business School, Boston, MA
Pauline A. Cochrane, Catholic University of America, Washington, DC
Dominique Coulombe, Brown University, Providence, RI
William J. Crowe, Ohio State University Libraries, Columbus, OH
Dana Cummings, The Berkshire Athenaeum, Pittsfield, MA
Doris Dale, Southern Illinois University, Carbondale, IL
Jane E. Edwards, State Law Library, Augusta, ME
Roy W. Evans, University of Missouri, Columbia, MO
Francine Feuerman, New York Public Library, New York, NY
Carol Fleishauer, MIT Libraries, Cambridge, MA
Mary Anne Fox, Southern Illinois University, Carbondale, IL
Ahmad Gamaluddin, Clarion University, Clarion, PA
Thomas Geoffino, Connecticut State Library, Hartford, CT

Jack D. Glazier, University of Missouri, Columbia, MO
Irene F. Glennon, Virginia Polytechnic Institute, Blacksburg, VA
Matthew Hartman, University of British Columbia, Vancouver, BC
Barry J. Hennessey, University of New Hampshire, Durham, NH
Marjorie Hess, Amherst College, Amherst, MA
Joseph A. Horn, Plymouth, MA
Carol Ishimoto, Harvard College Library, Cambridge, MA
Ling Hwey Jeng, University of Maryland, College Park, MD
Virginia Jing-yi Shih, ASIA, Alhambra, CA
Amy G. Job, Wm. Paterson College, Wayne, NJ
Sarah Hager Johnston, The Hartford Co., Hartford, CT
Doris Kammradt, University of Connecticut, Storrs, CT
Joanne Katsune, Brown University, Providence, RI
Kyle Kelly, New England School of Law, Boston, MA
Lawrence O. Kline, Duke University, Durham, NC
Karla S. Kuklis, McGill University, Montreal, QB
Helena Wang Lai, Bayside, NY
Tim Larson, Indiana University, Bloomington, IN
Michelle Lee, Labat-Anderson, Inc., Arlington, VA
Sul H. Lee, University of Oklahoma, Norman, OK
Dorcas Libby, Social Law Library, Boston, MA
Margaret Lourie, Harvard Law Library, Cambridge, MA
Frederick C. Lynden, Brown University, Providence, RI
Katha D. Massey, University of Georgia, Athens, GA
Marianne McGowan, Lesley College Libraries, Cambrdige, MA
Pamela Reekes McKirdy, Simmons College, Boston, MA
June Mullins, Tufts University, Medford, MA
Margaret Myers, American Library Association, Chicago, IL
Myrna Omansky, Digital Equipment Corp., Concord, MA
Freda E. Otchere, Concordia University, Montreal, QB
Marsha Starr Paiste, Salem, NH
Cecilia Piccolo, University of Arizona Library, Tucson, AZ
Susan Poteet, Southern Illinois University, Carbondale, IL
Diane M. Ranney, Sandwich, MA
Sally H. Reed, Bangor, ME
Norma F. Riddick, Vanderbilt University, Nasvhille, TN
Constance F. Roberts, University of Connecticut, Storrs, CT
Malka Schyndel, Lotus Development Corp., Cambridge, MA
Elizabeth Schreiber, Massachusetts General Hospital, Boston, MA
Nancy G. Serotkin, Falmouth, MA

Tseng-wen Shen, Reading, MA
Susan Sheridan, Amherst College Library, Amherst, MA
Sarah Thomas, National Agricultural Library, Beltsville, MD
David M. Turkalo, Social Law Library, Boston, MA
Carol White, University of Wyoming Library, Laramie, WY
M. Greg Whitney, Ecole Polytechnique de Montreal, Montreal, QB
Hugh Wilburn, Massachusetts Horticultural Society, Boston, MA
Adeline Wilkes, Texas Woman's University, Denton, TX
Maria Witt, Cite des Sciences et de l'Industrie, Paris, France
Helen Yeh, Prairie View A&M University, Prairie View, TX